kit **homes** modern

kit**homes**modern

Ima Ebong

COLLINS DESIGN

An Imprint of HarperCollinsPublishers

KIT HOMES MODERN.
Copyright © 2005 by GLITTERATI INCORPORATED
www.GlitteratiIncorporated.com

Text copyright © 2005 by Ima Ebong

HarperCollins books may be purchased for educational,
business, or sales promotional use. For information, please write:
Special Markets Department, HarperCollins Publishers,
10 East 53rd Street, New York, NY 10022.

FIRST EDITION

First published in 2005 by:
Collins Design
An Imprint of HarperCollinsPublishers
10 East 53rd Street
New York, NY 10022
Tel: (212) 207-7000
Fax: (212) 207-7654
collinsdesign@harpercollins.com
www.harpercollins.com

Distributed throughout the world by:
HarperCollinsPublishers
10 East 53rd Street
New York, NY 10022
Fax: (212) 207-7654

Design: Susi Oberhelman

Library of Congress Control Number: 2005931349

ISBN10: 0-06-082613-4
ISBN13: 978-0-06-082613-0

Printed and bound in China

1 2 3 4 5 6 7 / 11 10 09 08 07 06 05

FIRST PRINTING, 2005

contents

Living room, Adriance House, Brooklin, Maine, designed by Adam Kalkin

introduction

The homes featured in this volume are definitely not your grandfather's, or even your father's, prefab kit homes. Dispel memories of Sears mail-order kit houses, quaint Quonset Huts, do-it-yourself log cabins, or multi-gabled precut timber homes. The houses featured in this volume represent a new and improved version of prefab convenience architecture, one rooted more in the optimism and stylistic clarity of 20th-century modern design updated to suit 21st-century sensibilities—with the use of digital design tools and the latest building methods enriched by environmentally friendly sustainable materials.

The variety of designs featured here, not to mention the advanced construction methods employed, argue for a much wider definition of the kit house than the lingering stereotype of serviceable, bland do-it-yourself dwellings. The term "kit of parts" more accurately reflects the ambitious scope of the houses in this volume, which, together, make an important contribution to developing a more cost effective and systematic approach to residential housing construction. Leading the way, the architects in this volume, aided by the latest information-age computer technology, are creating a whole new plug-and-play design vocabulary comprised of interchangeable panels, modules, and linear components. In many ways, these various integrated approaches to home building have more in common with automotive and aircraft design than traditional residential construction.

A kit-of-parts approach to building, as architect, A. Scott Howe notes, relies on a highly organized, well-ordered, flexible system of pre-designed interchangeable parts, a sort of architectural mise en place, in which mass-produced standardized components seamlessly interface with each other, producing buildings unlimited in their creative scope and size. Kit-of-parts structures are easily transported as complete packages and more speedily assembled, ensuring not only cost efficiency, but also consistent results, reproducible in any environment. The kit-of-parts housing systems featured here are all the more remarkable for their adaptability. Room for individual expression is built into each project through a well-designed selection of mass-customized, interchangeable components.

From the outset, my intention was to profile only those modern kit homes currently in the marketplace and readily available for purchase. I quickly discovered, however, that there were worthy exceptions to the rule; prototypes that may never reach the market but that, nevertheless, offer particularly innovative examples of a kit-of-parts–based architecture. By no means exhaustive, this book has several noteworthy omissions, which unfortunately could not be included in time.

With the shortage of skilled labor and rising construction costs, kit-of-parts housing systems may well represent the home of the future. The sheer inventiveness and ingenuity of the work presented here certainly suggests that the future has arrived. ▪

Loftcube exterior, Berlin, Germany, designed by Studio Aisslinger

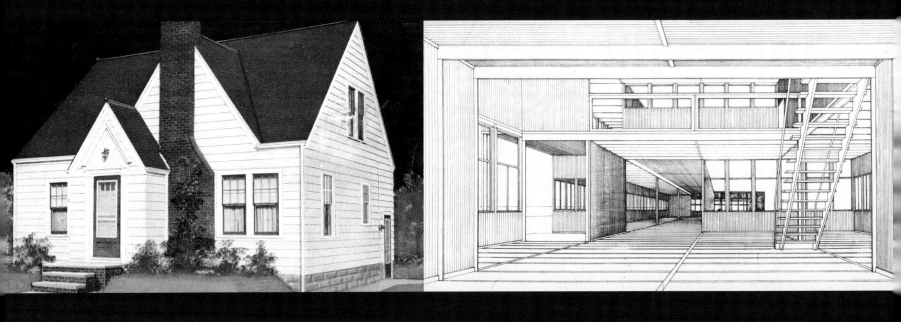

learning to box

a kit history

The dream of packaged kit houses purchased via mail-order catalogue or off-the-shelf has always been, in some respects, the holy grail of modern architecture. Some of the most famous modern architects of the 20th century, from Buckminster Fuller to Frank Lloyd Wright, invested enormous time and effort in pursuit of the ideal packaged kit house. The remains of many unsuccessful attempts are preserved in plans and sketches tucked away in the archives of many late great modern architects. Had they been successful, fans of modern architecture might well be in the delightful position of having to choose among an embarrassment of designer kit house riches branded with names like Frank Lloyd Wright, Mies van der Rohe, and Le Corbusier.

There are many reasons why most 20th-century modern architects failed in their attempt to create mass-produced prefabricated kits, where ventures such as the famous Sears mail-order houses succeeded. One reason seemed to be that in general, modern architects were never quite in the right place at the right time. They never seemed to find that "sweet spot" of time and circumstance, where design, technology, investment, production capacity, changing demographics, consumer demand, and marketing all worked in synch to produce spectacular results.

In the United States, consumer interest in prefabricated kit houses has always been greatest during moments of economic uncertainty, profound demographic change, and technological advances. The First World War in 1914 ushered in one such moment of heightened interest in prefab housing, when the need to house soldiers returning from battle and their families sparked interest in developing quickly built, affordable housing that could be instantly available for a rapidly expanding population. A second wave of interest in prefabricated kits occurred once again during the 1940s and lasted throughout the period of the Second World War, when once again speedily constructed affordable homes were urgently needed to house returning G.I.s, whose families would form the burgeoning Baby Boomer generation.

OPPOSITE: The vertiginous feel of this photograph, taken in 1945, reflects the dizzying pace at which the construction industry set about building homes to meet the acute post–World War II housing shortage. Comprised of a prefabricated kit of parts, the entire house was erected in 34 minutes according to *Life* magazine.

In the 21st century we are once again experiencing yet another resurgence of interest in prefabricated housing. This time attention appears to be driven less by the dramatic consequences of war, but instead by more subtle and quietly shifting economic and social patterns. The rising cost of housing is increasingly outpacing income, forcing families and first-time buyers (especially those living close to East and West coast metropolitan areas) to devote an increasingly larger portion of their earnings to housing. According to the United States Federal Housing Finance Board, the average purchase price of a single-family home reached $264,000 in 2004. With increasing financial burdens on the Baby Boomer generation, whether raising children, healthcare costs, caring for elderly parents, or planning for retirement, middle-class consumers are becoming increasingly aware of the need to bring lifestyle aspirations more in line with downward shifting economic realities. "Affordability with style" perhaps sums up a subtly growing lifestyle philosophy among urban professional Boomers and Generation Xers accustomed to the steady intravenous drip of enriched, mass-customized design, from flat-screen televisions and iPods to sleek-lined cars and assorted kitchen gadgets. Farsighted companies, among them Target, Ikea, Home Depot, and Jet Blue, have adjusted to consumer anxieties by building whole product lines and services on marketing stylish, affordable products to Boomers and Xers with great success. In contrast, the residential construction industry, always more conservative and wary of the fickle nature of the

housing consumer, has been, with some exception, slow to appreciate the growing niche of middle-class buyers who desire both affordability and good design. As the work presented in this volume shows, in an effort to fill the need for cost-effective, quality housing, a whole new crop of architects are traveling the well-worn path of prefabrication that predecessors such as Walter Gropius, Charles and Ray Eames, and other 20th-century architects once eagerly trod.

The first factory-made kit homes in the United States were developed in 1910 by Aladdin Homes of Bay City, a Michigan-based company credited with creating the first mail-order houses. The Aladdin company's kit homes were initially intended to serve as affordable vacation houses. Essentially the kits were simply made up of precut, numbered wood parts constructed as bungalows based on the then-popular Arts and Crafts style much admired for its timeless quality. Quickly erected in a day and some-times less, these early kit houses sold well and encouraged the company to expand its customer base to fill the rapidly expanding needs of the World War I generation. Savvy competitors like the famous Sears, Roebuck and Company quickly followed.

OPPOSITE: As this 1937 mail-order catalogue cover shows, ease of installation and assurances of product integrity were part of the consumer marketing of kit homes. ABOVE LEFT and RIGHT: The impressive variety of architectural styles and comforting familiarity of traditional designs assured the popularity of kits.

From the start, efficiency of production was key, and in its quest for speed and consistency Sears adopted assembly-line mass-production techniques modeled on Ford automobile factory methods. Once the customer made a catalogue mail-order purchase of a Sears kit home, the house was sent direct from the factory in precut numbered pieces packed in two box containers, which were shipped to their final destination by rail. The latest construction techniques used "Balloon style" framing, which cut construction time by forty percent and enabled houses to be quickly erected by one or two-man teams of carpenters who roamed from house to house to help customers put up their kit houses.

It would be misleading to portray Sears' achievements as representative of the entire picture in terms of early 20th-century housing innovation. During the 1920s and 1930s there were many parallel developments in domestic building. In fact, while Sears was beginning to slow down its production and trying to fend off the aftereffects of the Great Depression, an endless assortment of architects, manufacturing industries, commercial housing developers, and entrepreneurs created prefabricated housing kit prototypes with the hope of inventing the one silver bullet that would solve the housing crisis.

Among other factory-made housing models, trailers were an increasingly popular affordable housing alternative from the 1920s onward. Initially mobile homes served the needs of practical, cost-conscious travelers who combined the desire to experience the great American outdoors with a ready-made place to stay. By the time World War II loomed, mobile trailers began to be used for purposes other than travel. They became larger in size and were often used to house factory workers as well as temporary housing for veterans and their families. The mobile home's stationary status was symbolized by the familiar sight of the vehicle, with missing wheels, hoisted on a more permanent foundation of cement cinder blocks. The negative image that trailers have long endured often obscures their success in delivering cost-effective housing alternatives bolstered by a highly effective marketing and distribution system. While mobile homes leave a lot to be desired design-wise, their consumer-friendly marketing, distribution, and delivery systems may be a worthy model to explore for today's modern kit homes.

With the end of World War II, the chronic housing shortage that ensued had to be addressed. Indeed it was made all the more urgent by the need to provide homes for returning soldiers. A 1940 issue of *The Forum* magazine noted, "The end of the Second World War

OPPOSITE: As mobile homes evolved from recreational vehicles to more permanent dwellings, piers replaced wheels as stabilizers. It would take several federal statutes to mandate disaster-proof, permanent foundations as well as a change of name from mobile home to manufactured house before these affordable homes eventually acquired the look of traditional domestic dwellings.

ushered in a boom in prefabs using new materials and methods developed during the war years. Most pressing was the need to house returning soldiers and their growing families, which spurred the second wave of interest developing mass-produced factory built home kits." The initiative belonged not to modern architects but to savvy business men like Bill Levitt, the genius behind the large-scale housing developments of Levittown, who saw the coming need for housing and swiftly stepped in to fill it.

The first Levittown development was created in 1947 in Long Island, New York. Using the unrelenting efficiency of updated factory assembly techniques, mass-produced cookie-cutter kit houses were created for the lowest possible cost. Every part of the house, from precut wood planks to nails, was standardized

and churned out at a factory according to exacting specifications. Housing parts were packed in a container and trucked to the 1,400-acre Levittown housing development, where scores of workers, aided by construction machinery, formed the largest outdoor work site, erecting house after house in neat, monotonous identical rows. Perhaps realizing the potential sterility of assembly-line sameness, Levitt cleverly created some of the earliest post-war urban planned settlements by surrounding his formulaic mass-produced kit homes with parks, wide streets, pavements, and areas to congregate and play.

Another prefabricated factory-made solution created to alleviate the post–World War II housing crunch was the Lustron kit house, a steel-paneled structure created between 1946 and 1947 by inventor and engineer Carl Stradlund. Lustrons, which today are enjoying something of a revival, came in beguiling pastel shades of blue, yellow, gray, and beige. Shipped as a kit of parts, the disassembled house was packed into one large container and transported directly from the factory to the site by truck. Each house included a washing machine, an innovative built-in radiant heating system, a dishwasher, and furniture. The skeletal frame was made of steel to which wall sections were welded. The roof, as well as the exterior and interior walls, was made out of interlocking steel panels coated with a porcelain enamel finish sprayed on at the factory. For all the positive publicity and consumer interest, supply could not keep up with demand—a recurring

OPPOSITE: This 1948 Levittown housing development in New York was a marvel of efficiency. Prebuilt components such as staircases, fencing, cabinets, and appliances added to the speed of construction. ABOVE: Photographer Margaret Bourke-White's aerial view of the housing development in Levittown, Pennsylvania, reveals the clever asymmetrical layout designed to lessen the impact of rows of identical houses.

kit homes modern

problem that would nip at the heels of prefab kit manufacturers in the 1940s. The company was plagued by a toxic combination of ruthless competitors and chronic production problems resulting in backorders and even a few lawsuits. Consumer interest eventually waned once the housing crisis had been alleviated by the late 1940s. In 1951 the Lustron factory closed it doors for good and Carl Stradlund's dream of the factory-made kit house was effectively mothballed.

Due to Circumstances Beyond Our Control. . .

While traditional-looking mass-produced housing kits bearing names like Sears, Lustron, and Levitt were being hailed as miracle solutions to the housing crises between the war years, modern architects were still struggling to put their own stamp on the domestic housing crisis. Though they tried hard to come up with prefabricated homes created with the latest machine-age technology, the modernist road to the factory-built kit house ended up being littered with abandoned prototypes. Among the many reasons that modern architects failed to make a lasting impact in the notoriously difficult area of factory-built prefab housing was the nature of the competition architects faced. Though the 1940s was a period of time when easily available government loans and tax incentives made it favorable for architects to get into the housing business, the field of factory-made housing was occupied by a tight amalgam of tough, highly competitive business interests made up of

property developers, industrialists, and assorted manufacturers who were anxious to generate new markets for their raw material. Like an unfortunate passenger stuck in the back seat of a car with larger companions, modern architects tended to be wedged in between commercial interests that often left little room to maneuver. It is notable that a businessman/property developer and an

OPPOSITE: Photographed by Arnold Newman in 1949, portraits like this Lustron "exploded house" reveal the compact, convenient all-inclusive packaging of Lustron kit houses, which could be made turnkey ready in a day. ABOVE: The Lustron house was famous for its exterior cladding, made of metal sheets sprayed with a smooth enamel finish that required little maintenance.

engineer/entrepreneur were the ones who initiated mass-produced housing kit projects like Levittown and Lustron. Unlike architects, commercial developers and businessmen seemed more nimble, more able to step back from their projects and evaluate problems with the unvarnished bottom line in mind. In contrast, for many of the key modern architects who tried their hand at prefab mass housing, design integrity was the only bottom line. With the exception of a few committed developers like Joseph Eichler, who sought out the best modern architects for his housing projects, it seemed that for more commercially minded property entrepreneurs modernism was not an article of faith but a marketing strategy useful along with the latest General Electric appliances and kitchen cabinets as a means of enticing consumers. For modern architects on the other hand, good design was key and could not be separated from issues of affordability or construction technology.

Walter Gropius, the highly regarded modern architect and a founder of the famous Bauhaus art school (the leading school of modern architecture and incubator of 20th-century modernism) in Germany,

had long been fascinated by the possibilities of applying innovative industrial techniques to create mass-produced housing kits. While Sears was equipping its traditional homes with precut timber frames and historical flourishes, Gropius, as early as 1910 had begun to think about factory-prefabricated houses made from materials such as steel.

In 1942 Gropius and Wachsmann formed the General Panel Corporation hoping to capitalize on their extensive knowledge of prefabrication and Konrad Wachsmann's advanced panel system. The company's first project was the Packaged House System, a kit home created from a system of framed wood panels. The first prototypes were created in 1943; they had hoped to produce 10,000 houses a year and received loans with that schedule as a target. Unfortunately, as Gilbert Herbert's authoritative account of Gropius and Wachsmann's struggles documents (see *The Dream of The Factory-Made House*), there were problems along the way, ranging from bad factory equipment to Wachsmann's tendency to get sidetracked in his quest for perfection. Halfway through production of the Packaged House, Wachsmann could not resist tweaking the system; he became distracted by the possibilities of incorporating new materials such as plastic and metal framing for the panels. To compound matters, neither Wachsmann nor Gropius were involved or experienced enough in the sales and marketing side of the housing business. By 1948 they managed to produce and sell just fifteen houses, but by then the housing shortage crisis was

OPPOSITE: Walter Gropius and Konrad Wachsmann's factory-made standardized panels served as the basic building blocks of his Packaged House System. The wood floor and wall panels created a multi-story framing system resulting in freestanding interior spaces with flexible wall partitions.

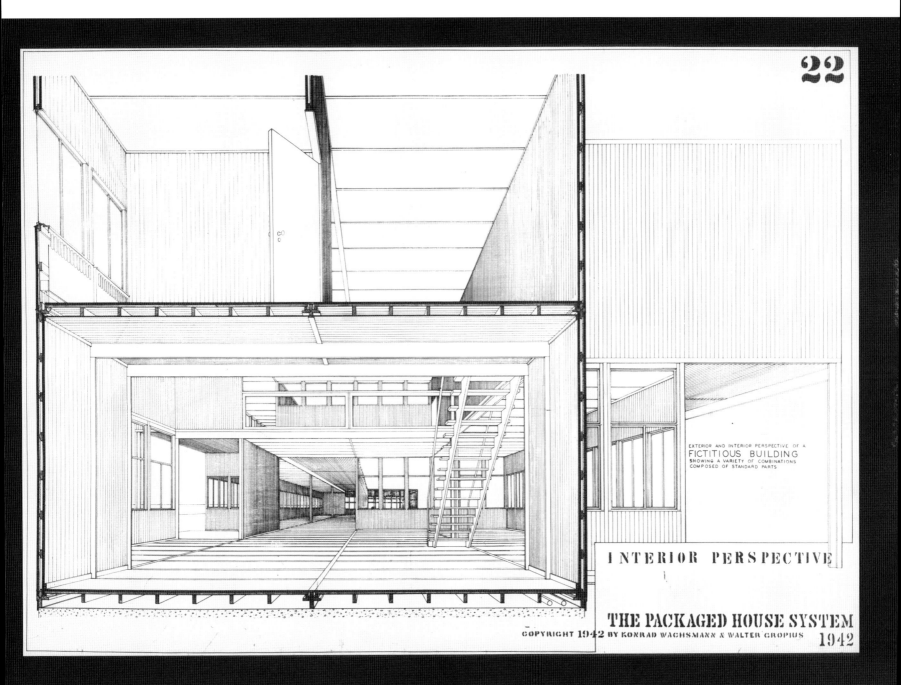

22

EXTERIOR AND INTERIOR PERSPECTIVE OF A
FICTITIOUS BUILDING
SHOWING A VARIETY OF COMBINATIONS
COMPOSED OF STANDARD PARTS

INTERIOR PERSPECTIVE

THE PACKAGED HOUSE SYSTEM
COPYRIGHT 1942 BY KONRAD WACHSMANN & WALTER GROPIUS   1942

beginning to improve and correspondingly interest in factory-made packaged kits peaked. Consumer tastes were beginning to return to more conventional housing. In 1951, the General Panel Corporation was liquidated and yet again the dream of the factory-made house was postponed indefinitely.

As far back as the turn of the 20th century, Frank Lloyd Wright had troubled himself with the challenge of creating affordable housing. Although Wright's best-known effort was his Usonian prefabricated houses, less well-known were some of his last prefabricated kit homes created in 1957 for Marshall Erdman, a design-savvy owner of a construction company Marshall Erdman & Associates. A rarity in the bottom-line motivated building industry, Erdman, like fellow developer Joseph Eichler, was open to trying out ideas that combined modern aesthetics with affordability. Wright persuaded Erdman that he could create affordable, well-designed prefabricated kit houses for $15,000, half the cost of Erdman's then-existing "U-Form-It" kit homes. Perhaps sensing the irresistible opportunity to market a line of affordable houses stamped with the brand name of America's best-known architect, Erdman took up Wright's offer.

The first Erdman prefabs, as they were commonly called, were built in 1955 and based on three designs. The most interesting was Erdman Prefab Design #2, a compact light-filled prefab kit constructed in 1957 in Madison, Wisconsin. Its square shape contained a double-height living room flanked

by a perpendicular wall of rectangular wood-framed ribbon windows that bathed the house in natural light and made for an effective passive solar system. The windows also engaged with the surrounding

OPPOSITE, LEFT ABOVE: Frank Lloyd Wright's Erdman Prefab Design # 2, also known as the Rudin Residence, incorporated many of the architect's signature elements including ribbon windows. **OPPOSITE, LEFT BELOW:** Horizontal paneling creates a feeling of spaciousness and clerestory windows filter natural light. **OPPOSITE, RIGHT BELOW:** Wright's stylish furniture was an integral part of the interior. **OPPOSITE, RIGHT ABOVE:** The built-in kitchen looks as fresh and appealing today as it did in the 1950s. **ABOVE:** Wright's famous textile block pattern forms a decorative frieze around the roofline.

ABOVE: Charles and Ray Eames's Case Study House #8 featured a light steel frame that created a soaring full-height sitting room framed by industrial plate glass, blurring the boundary between indoor and outdoor spaces. OPPOSITE: Drawings for the do-it-yourself Kwikset reveal a well-thought-out, easily assembled prefabricated home. The flexible kit of parts included wood panels, sliding glass doors, and movable internal partitions.

greenery maintaining, even at the affordable end of the scale, Wright's organic, environmentally friendly principles. Standardized panels of mahogany lined the interior, and the roofline was capped with Wright's decorative molded blocks, which added visual texture and richness to the home. The house arrived as a kit of parts complete with components from kitchen cabinets to windows and exterior walls—everything needed to complete the house save for the foundation, heating and plumbing fixtures, electrical wiring, and paint, all of which the buyer had to supply.

Despite the prestige and innovation Wright brought to the project, the Erdman prefab homes proved simply too expensive to produce and were never cost-effective enough to attract lower-income buyers. In the end, despite major publicity in architectural journals and newsweeklies like *Time* and *Life*, only eleven kits were sold. The average cost of an Erdman prefab in 1959 was $20,000 for materials and $35,000 for construction. Although they were among the most beautiful and livable prefab kit houses of their day, the Wright houses in the end were simply not affordable enough. Erdman lost money on the venture and had to stop making the prefabs kits by 1959.

Charles and Ray Eames, the famous 20th-century husband-and-wife architect and design team, also tried to create an innovative home building system that relied on a kit of parts. Their iconic Case Study House #8 represented a bold development in off-the-shelf housing and was a living laboratory of sorts in which the creative possibilities inherent in industrial materials and components were exuberantly explored

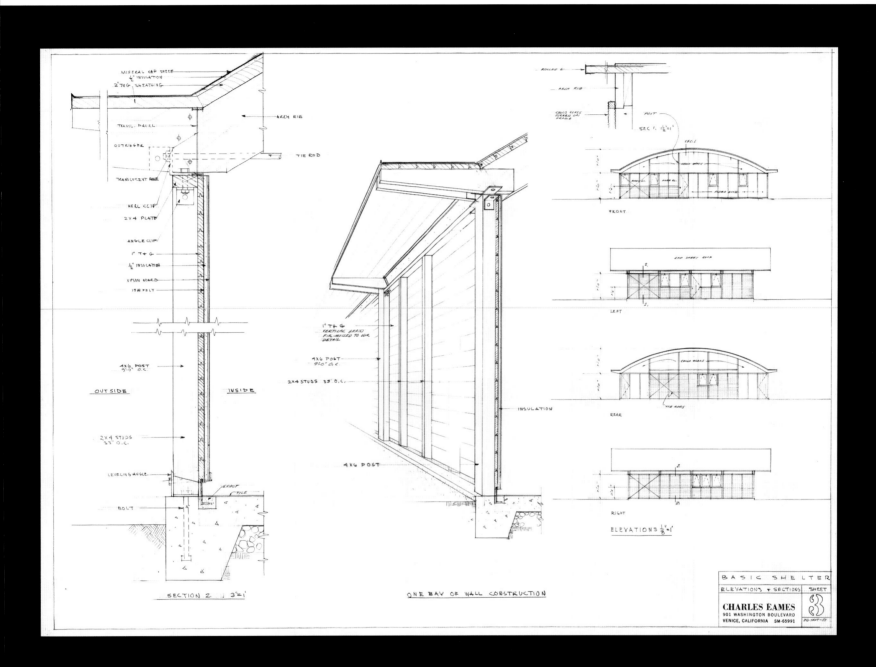

MINERAL CAP SHEET
4" INSULATION
2" T&G. SHEATHING

ARCH RIB

TRANSL. PANEL

OUTRIGGER

TIE ROD

TRANSLUCENT PANEL

HEEL CLIP

2×4 PLATE

ANGLE CLIP

1" T & G

½" INSULATION

UPSON BOARD

15# FELT

4×6. POST
5'-0" O.C.

OUTSIDE

INSIDE

2×4 STUDS
33" O.C.

LEVELING ANGLE

GROUT
TILE

BOLT

SECTION 2. 3"=1'

ROLLED L

ARCH RIB

CHECO SCREWS
FRAMED ON
FRAME

POST

SEC 1, 1½"=1'

T&G.L

CHECO WIRED

PANEL EL.

FIXED WIRED

FRONT

CAP SHEET EDGE

LEFT

CHECO WIRES

TIE RODS

REAR

RIGHT

ELEVATIONS ⅛"=1'

1" T & G
VERTICAL GRAIN
FIR-MILLED TO 1¼"
DETAIL

4×6 POST
5'0" O.C.

2×4 STUDS 33" O.C.

INSULATION

4×6 POST

ONE BAY OF WALL CONSTRUCTION

BASIC SHELTER	
ELEVATIONS + SECTIONS	SHEET
CHARLES EAMES 901 WASHINGTON BOULEVARD VENICE, CALIFORNIA SM-65991	23

in the context of the practical realities of everyday life. Case Study House #8 was an important precursor to a new prefabricated kit house, which the architects called the Kwikset. As the plans and drawings reveal, the unbuilt house was an imaginative and sophisticated mix of glass, wood, and steel. Had the Kwikset been realized, it would have made a wonderful follow-up to Case Study House #8. The design demonstrated that standardized factory-made components need not result in sterile, endlessly replicated static designs, but instead could result in flexible kit of parts that could allow architects to more playfully and efficiently explore an endless combination of creative housing options. Sadly the Kwikset house project never got past the drawing board. Other Case Study House architects like Pierre Koenig created innovative prototypes that also pointed the way to using mass-producible factory fabricated industrial components to create beautifully designed affordable modern homes. Koenig's 1959 Case Study House #21 was essentially composed of a kit of parts containing steel frames and beams as well as concrete and glass panels.

In the 1950s and 1960s, some of the most imaginative modern kit houses were built as vacation homes. Easily broken down into precut, factory-made standardized parts, an entire home could be trans-

LEFT: Set in the hills overlooking Los Angeles, Pierre Koenig's Case Study House #21 was created from manufactured steel and glass industrial components. Meticulously integrated detailing such as the brick patio and cooling water pools created a rich tapestry of sight, sound, and texture, offsetting the muted simplicity of the architecture itself.

1967 Danish-born architect and furniture designer Jens Risom designed his holiday home as a prefabricated kit, easily transportable to its remote windy site at the northern end of Block Island, where winds sometimes reached 100 miles per hour. Beautifully crafted, the elegant kit cost all of $20,000 and included precut lumber sections, lighting fixtures, and kitchen and bath fixtures—quite a bargain by 1960s standards. The house's kit of numbered parts made it easy to erect on the remote island with few skilled laborers. Risom's finely crafted kit house is an example of the high-quality aesthetic values that modern architects held onto in a sea of cheaply made mass-produced prefab kits that sprouted up in housing developments.

The Future of the Kit House in a Plug-and-Play World

New building techniques and materials are expanding the possibilities of kit houses, especially in terms of creating more cost-efficient packaged systems. With the growing industrialization of housing construction, architects are increasingly open to the benefits of technology transfer and exploring advanced design and fabrication techniques used in the airline, shipping, and automobile industries. As authors Stephen Kieran and James Timberlake have argued in *Refabricating Architecture*, there is a lot that the building industry can learn from automotive and aerospace industries, which have long since abandoned the compartmentalized, hierarchical, top-down, linear

homes. Easily broken down into precut, factory-made standardized parts, an entire home could be transported in pieces on the back of a truck for quick assembly on-site with little more than a two-man team. In

OPPOSITE: Like the furniture designs for which he is famous, Jens Risom's compact timber-framed kit house featured the warmth of wood and combined it with a pristine, modern, light-filled open-plan space. ABOVE: The kit layout reveals an impressive architectural *mise en place* consisting of precut factory-made components including timber planks, glass sheets, and built-in cabinets.

production methods so prone to miscommunication, waste, and costly error. The organizational systems of industrial conglomerates such as Toyota, Airbus, BMW, and Boeing, to name a few, have long favored collective digitally managed design and production processes with simultaneous input across the board from designers, engineers, and material specialists among other contributors. The latest 840-seat, double-decker Airbus A380 plane, for example, was created largely off-site using advanced modular production techniques. By the time it was ready for assembly the Airbus A380 consisted of just six main components: the 240-foot fuselage was created in parts, the rear section was made in Germany and the front and central sections were made in France, the horizontal portion of the tail was made in Spain, and the 261-foot wings were made in England. The six components were shipped by a combination of RoRo (roll-on roll-off) ferry, barge, and trailer truck to their final destination

ABOVE, OPPOSITE TOP and BOTTOM: With an eye on reducing costs and maintaining quality, advanced component-based manufacturing techniques were used to create the Airbus A380 super plane. The wings, fuselage, and nose of the Airbus were developed off-site in different European countries and then shipped by air, road, and water to the main Airbus factory in Toulouse, France, for final assembly.

at the main Airbus factory in Toulouse, France, where the sections were finally assembled. Not only is a component-based manufacturing system cheaper, faster, and more efficient, it is also less prone to error, since each separate off-site entity serves as a "center of excellence" (see Al Schuler's "Industrialization in Housing," *Structural Building Components Magazine*, March 2002) that focuses exclusively on its own piece of the puzzle, without getting distracted by the big picture.

In the construction industry basic modular techniques have long been employed in the commercial construction of bland, serviceable buildings such as hotels, fast-food restaurants, hospitals, dormitories, and offices. Widespread use of modular construction in housing only began in earnest in the 1970s. Unfortunately, in the hands of mainstream builders modular construction has only served the most mundane of goals—to produce faster and more efficient cookie-cutter traditional-style homes. As many of the architects featured in this volume show, modular construction methods can produce exciting design.

Some of the most vibrant experimentation in prefabricated housing is taking place in Europe, particularly in Austria, the Netherlands, and Britain, and is fueled in part by a traditional commitment to creating affordable social housing. Raines Court, an award-winning apartment building designed by the noted British firm of Allford Hall Monaghan Morris is one example of the ongoing experimentation in modular design. The apartment complex, located in

London, consists of 127 rectangular steel-framed modules skillfully joined together to create one-, two-, and three-bedroom high-quality apartment units. Not unlike airplane or automobile fabrication, the fully decorated modules, complete with built-in partitions, insulation, wiring, plumbing, kitchens, and bathrooms, were created off-site in a factory then transported to their final destination by truck, where they were then hoisted into place by crane. Although the entire experimental apartment complex was built in ten months, longer than the optimal four months, the imaginative linking of preassembled, outfitted modules to create livable space marks an important example of how modular design may impact the kit house, which today is just as likely to be delivered as an empty shell or series of modules that the owner may choose to finish to their satisfaction.

Another example of innovative modular design is the Spacebox, a series of self-contained studio apartment units created by De Vijf, an innovative Dutch architecture firm. The benefits of technology transfer can be seen in the outer shell, made from a high-grade composite used in shipping and aircraft construction. The 193-square-foot studio residence contains kitchen, toilet, and shower facilities; the modules are delivered preassembled complete with electricity, telephone, Internet, and plumbing connections in place. An imaginative temporary solution to housing shortages, the Spacebox is currently used as multiunit dormitories for students at various universities throughout Holland.

ABOVE: The experimental Raines Court apartment complex in London, England, was built completely off-site in a factory. The fully furnished modules, including kitchens and bathrooms, were trucked to the site and then hoisted into place by crane. OPPOSITE TOP and BOTTOM: Designed by the Dutch architecture firm De Vijf, Spacebox temporary student housing is easily plugged into place by crane. Studio modules come fully equipped with a shower, kitchen, toilet, heating, ventilation, and telephone lines.

housing industry, modern architects working today, unlike their counterparts in the 1940s and 1950s, have an unprecedented opportunity to bring their ideas to the marketplace. With no acute housing crisis to reward speed of construction over good design, and with modernism now viewed in historical if not nostalgic terms, rather than the novelty it was in the post war years, today's architects have the luxury of time and more favorable circumstance when compared with their modernist predecessors. The Internet is also proving to be an effective leveler of the playing field and an important marketing tool through which architects can reach a dedicated audience directly.

Architects like Frank Lloyd Wright and Walter Gropius, though at opposite ends of the modern architecture spectrum, believed passionately in the life-enhancing potential of prefabrication as a sustainable housing system—in other words, as a means to more means, not the devalued and impoverished architecture-of-last-resort that came to be associated with prefabs. The variety of houses featured in this book reveals a new dynamism at work among the latest generation of architects. Despite the endless cookie-cutter mutations, which still define much of the prefabricated housing industry, and which once diminished their predecessor's dreams, architects today are once again at the forefront of engineering new ways of living. ■

CHAPTER 2

the profiles

far horizon

CUTLER ANDERSON ARCHITECTS

Far Horizon is the result of a unique partnership between the internationally recognized, Seattle-based firm of Cutler Anderson Architects and Lindal Cedar Homes, the largest manufacturer and supplier of packaged-home kits in the United States.

James Cutler, principal and founder of Cutler Anderson Architects, is particularly admired for his elegant, environmentally sensitive buildings that embrace the landscape. His residential architecture in particular has won fulsome praise as "some of the most finely wrought timber-frame houses in the nation." Though Cutler has a distinguished body of work to his name, comprising more than three hundred projects spread over three continents, he is best known to the public for Xanadu, the 40,000-square-foot Pacific Northwest residence of Microsoft founder Bill Gates, overlooking Lake Washington in Washington State. At 2,890 square feet, Far Horizon is considerably smaller, though no less filled with the same rigor and design integrity of Cutler's larger-scale work. The three-bedroom home has the distinct aesthetic of a custom-built Cutler

RIGHT: The siting of the Far·Horizon among sycamore trees reflects the attention to environmental preservation. The natural stone foundation blends in with the surrounding landscape. At night the house appears to hover over the land rather than dominate it.

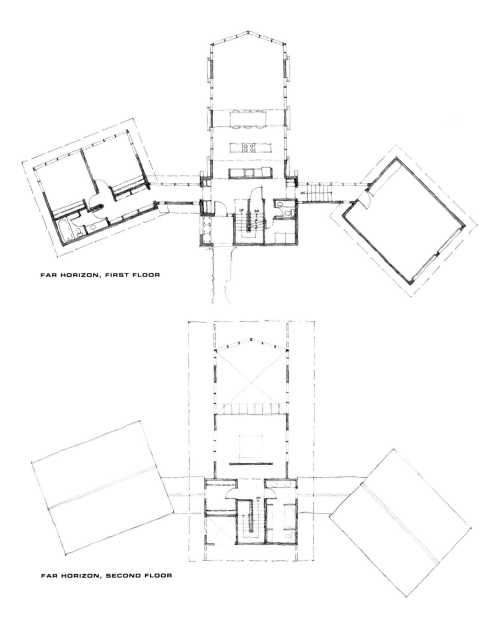

FAR HORIZON, FIRST FLOOR

FAR HORIZON, SECOND FLOOR

ABOVE: Placed on either side of the house, insulated glass corridors connect ancillary rooms with the main core. The flexible wings can be positioned to suit a variety of views and terrain. **OPPOSITE:** Far Horizon's post-and-beam framing system allows the creation of soaring, light-filled open spaces in the great room, and provides uninterrupted views of the lake and trees.

Anderson residence. The difference is in the packaging: The ultimate luxury modern kit house, Far Horizon comes neatly and conveniently packaged with ready-made precut and numbered timber parts, eliminating not only the lengthy process of commissioning a Cutler Anderson house from scratch but also a lot of the cost associated with custom-designed projects.

Cutler's deft reinterpretation of the traditional pitch roof post-and-beam home is altogether more streamlined and has a lighter touch. The elegant and restrained wood skeletal frame that defines Far Horizon's dramatic floor-to-ceiling glass-fronted prow interacts with the land instead of dominating it. Entry occurs via the rear elevation and leads to the foyer, which in turn connects to the 1,014-square-foot first-floor space, defined by an open-plan kitchen, dining, and living area. The dining section segues into an impressive double-height great room with a cathedral ceiling that rises to twenty-seven feet at its peak. The wall of windows supported by a post-and-beam skeletal frame allow sweeping 180-degree views of Missouri's Alpine Lake below in addition to copious light. The second floor is a 728-square-foot loft space, which, except for a bathroom located at the rear, is otherwise devoted entirely to the master bedroom suite. The loft bedroom overlooks the dining space and great room below and enjoys commanding views through the glass-walled prow to the lake beyond.

Attached to the main core of the house are two insulated glass-framed walkways, or links. The adjoining

arms, placed on either side of the main house, connect the separate wings to the main core. On one side, the glass-enclosed link leads to the wing containing a study, laundry room, and two-car garage. On the opposite side of the main core, the other walkway leads to the wing housing a second and third bedroom with a bath to share. Two discrete cedar decks flank either side of the main house and are accessible from the outside via stone steps as well as through wood-framed glass double doors placed just off the kitchen area on opposite sides of the core.

Cutler's modernist sensibility and belief in truth-in-materials is reflected in the exposed inner workings

LEFT: The beautifully ordered open plan creates elegant transitions between the kitchen, dining, and living areas. The exquisite detailing is visible in leaf-pattern motifs inlaid in the wood paneling above the first floor. ABOVE: The wood and stone deck forms a discreet platform for viewing the scenery.

The meticulously crafted bolts, metal connectors, and rods reveal the inner life of the house—very much a Cutler Anderson signature.

The clarity of Cutler Anderson's vision and rigorous attention to detail is evident inside and out, and are characteristics one normally associates with a custom-designed home. The exacting design is impressive and in many ways pushes the post-and-beam kit house to a new level, fulfilling both Cutler Anderson and Lindal's goal to bring the more prohibitive cost of custom home construction within reach of design-savvy homebuyers who might not otherwise be able to afford the design services of a leading architecture firm. The Far Horizon show house overlooks the expansive 236-acre Alpine Lake and is located in the upscale vacation resort community of Innsbrook, Missouri. According to the Innsbrook Properties sales sheet, the Far Horizon show house is priced at $979,000.

The firm's reputation for exacting detail extends to the siting of the kit house. After a Far Horizon kit has been purchased, the Lindal dealer supplies the architects with detailed photographs of the buyer's property along with site plans in order to study the best possible place to position the home on its lot. For architect James Cutler, the placement of a house is critical and can make or break the overall design. The importance given to the site also reflects Cutler's respect for the environment. The pragmatic consideration of passive energy and other site-specific aspects are seamlessly fused with a great reverence for the

of the house. Like turning over a finely crafted cello, at various points throughout the house a sense of the structure at work can be glimpsed in sightings of exposed beams and galvanized tension rods, which act as roof supports and are clearly visible in the great room, master bedroom, and other parts of the house.

ABOVE LEFT: The exquisite detailing extends to the hardware. Reveal Designs, a partner company of Cutler Anderson Architects, created the elegant stainless steel and cherry wood door levers. ABOVE RIGHT: Even the structural supports are meticulously finished; bolts connecting an internal steel plate between timber frames are capped by smoothened round metal plugs. OPPOSITE: The streamlined open kitchen elegantly combines sleek modern stainless steel appliances with the warmth of wood cabinets.

land inspired in part by the architect's early years working with Louis I. Kahn. For Cutler, nature is not merely a decorative foil for a building, instead, the key is to find that essential point of entry in the landscape where a house can be gently inserted into nature, thereby becoming a very part of the environment.

Lindal Cedar Homes, which manufactures and sells the Far Horizon kit as part of its Reflections Home Series, offers buyers a highly flexible package in tune with the growth and contraction of today's family cycle. Depending on the terrain, size of the lot, and the regional cost of labor, the main core of the house can be sold separately for around $300,000, giving buyers the option of adding wings later. The highly adaptable wings can also be rotated and positioned to take advantage of diverse views, including terrain as varied as desert or woodland. The wings are also responsive to the changing mix of family life; the garage addition can be used as an extra bedroom or a media room and equally, the bedroom wing can be changed into a study or independent living quarters for parents or older children.

The interior of the Far Horizon show house is designed in subtle, restrained tones. According to Steve Patton, a co-owner of Patton Interiors, the St. Louis firm responsible for the interior design, the inspiration for the color scheme came from the bark of the sycamore tree, prevalent throughout the wooded lake-front property. The interior is a symphony of understated global elegance, from Asian decorative

influences to Mission-style furniture and contemporary leather dining chairs. The subtle shades of green and gray play well against the wood and stone without competing for attention of the view beyond. ▪

OPPOSITE: The master bedroom loft is decorated in muted colors inspired by the green-gray tones of the sycamore trees. A steel tension rod reveals the inner workings of the house. ABOVE: The pleasure in materials is expressed in the bathroom's elegant wood cabinets, floors, and sink countertop.

glidehouse

MICHELLE KAUFMANN DESIGNS

"It's the real deal," reported a Glidehouse owner who belatedly visited the prefab at an open house only months after she purchased it. As the owner cautioned, it is probably not advisable to buy a house on the basis of images alone, but at the time of her purchase, the Glidehouse existed only on paper. The homeowner's leap of faith, however, seems to have been amply rewarded.

ABOVE and RIGHT: The elegant, elongated façade is framed by large sliding doors, which span the entire house and draw in natural light. A horizontal wood-screen cover glides over the glass sliding doors, providing shade. The tilt-up roof allows for spacious interiors with high ceilings and good ventilation.

An uninterrupted series of sliding glass doors frame the front elevation and are designed to effortlessly glide open and shut—hence the name Glidehouse. The glass doors also blur the division between indoor and outdoor areas, drawing in natural light while embracing the panoramic view outside. An extra sliding wood screen with horizontal slats forms an extra cover over the glass doors, providing an additional layer for privacy while allowing adequate ventilation. In contrast to the openness of the glass-framed façade, the exterior side and rear elevations are clad in Galvalume corrugated metal sheets, which shield the more private parts of the house.

The 1,344-square-foot, two-bedroom version of the Glidehouse show house consists of two modules, each 14 feet wide by 48 feet long. The length of a module is an industry standard determined by the maximum size that can be placed on a flatbed truck. The two modules are set in a staggered parallel, allowing for patio space adjacent to the rear bedroom and in front of the master bedroom. The appeal to "clean living" and a streamlined, uncluttered modern aesthetic influences practical matters of storage. A cleverly arranged storage wall, which runs the full length of the house, is located opposite the sliding doors. This storage bar is concealed by handsome plywood sliding doors overlaid with a birch veneer and is available in three different color stains. The storage doors are also available in white, although the wood adds warmth and emphasizes the house's natural

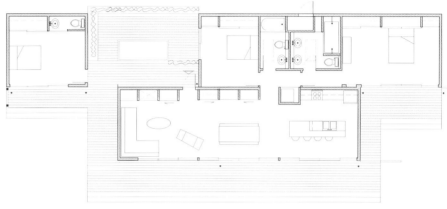

GLIDEHOUSE, FIRST FLOOR

ambiance. The storage area is highly flexible and can be arranged to suit the needs of the homeowner. Different parts of the storage bar can be configured to hold a range of household items such as books and clothing, electronic media, or kitchen utensils. Alternatively, the storage wall can simply be removed to provide additional space in the living and dining area. The rear module contains the private zones and consists of a master bedroom as well as an additional smaller bedroom; both have adjoining bathrooms and patios. A clerestory window strip runs along the rear elevation, providing extra light and promoting cross ventilation.

OPPOSITE: The open-plan kitchen and dining area has a spare, modern look enriched by environmentally friendly bamboo floors and birch kitchen cabinets. The sliding doors create a light-filled spacious interior.

ABOVE: A space-saving built-in shelf desk provides workspace. OPPOSITE: Partially open birch veneer doors form part of an extensive built-in "space bar" storage area incorporated into the wall opposite the sliding doors.

The approachable design of the Glidehouse in many ways is all the more remarkable for its ability to unsentimentally draw upon a comforting memory pool of American regional architectural styles, recasting them in a more contemporary and universal language. Kaufmann herself has mentioned Japanese domestic architecture, Joseph Eichler, and Charles and Ray Eames along with the rural farm buildings of her Iowa childhood among her influences. There is a resonance with all these elements, whether it is the Japanese-like feel of the sliding screens, the open airy domestic informality reminiscent of an Eichler, the horizontal low pitch of an arts and crafts bungalow, or the corrugated steel exterior that celebrates both Case Study style and farm shed aesthetics. Despite its modernity, there is something vaguely familiar about Glidehouse. A comforting déjà vu sensibility permeates the design, which perhaps helps to explain, in part, why the Glidehouse is universally popular with young and old buyers alike and equally at home in the suburbs as it is in rural settings.

Kaufmann often likens the Glidehouse to a Toyota Prius hybrid car and has made green living an overall part of the Glidehouse design philosophy. The architect collaborated with the Eagle Institute Design to create special insulation to minimize mold and allow minimum loss of heat. Greater energy efficiency is available as an optional extra and includes a choice of solar panels, wind generator, or a combination hybrid system. Glidehouse's interior finishes are sustainable,

glidehouse

too, and include bamboo flooring (a popular alternative to timber, bamboo forests are more quickly replenished than other wood varieties), and countertops made with recycled materials.

Among the benefits of modular construction is the ease of mass customization evident in the various Glidehouse floor plans offered by the architect. The factory-made, 14-by-48-foot rectangular standard module forms the basic shell, which like the chassis of a car serves as the framework for a variety of designs. The Glidehouse comes in two-, three-, and four-bedroom versions measuring between 1,344 and 2,240 square feet and modules can be configured in response to the shape of the site. Currently, Kaufmann is working on a two-story version of the Glidehouse, more suited to more dense urban and suburban lots where a sliver of land may be all that is available. The introduction of new versions of Glidehouse feels more like a brand, always vital and responsive to new materials, technologies, and consumer needs, not unlike the periodic update of the next generation of a design product. Like any well-designed and marketed product, the consumer is kept engaged by a whole host of upgrades and add-ons, from the choice of new interior and exterior finishes, to stylish add-ons such as carports and decks. Modular kit homes like the Glidehouse are changing the way modern prefab homes are marketed. As Kaufman unabashedly notes, "The current real estate market demonstrated to us that there are very few options available to people like

ourselves and our friends for a new type of housing alternative. . . . We feel we've done for prefabricated homes what Ikea has done for furniture and Volkswagen has done for cars, which translates to intelligent design at affordable prices." ▪

OPPOSITE: Clerestory windows above the bed ensure good cross ventilation and built-in birch veneer closets and cabinets are seamlessly incorporated into the storage space. A slim rectangular box dress mirror fits neatly in the corner. The external wood louver screen blocks harsh sunlight. ABOVE LEFT and RIGHT: Copper gray slate tile on the bathroom floor and shower walls reflects the thoughtful use of natural materials throughout the house.

branford point

FACE DESIGN

With its distinctive arched steel frame, Branford Point forms a visual contrast to the box shape of many modular kit houses. The house is an important example of the benefits of steel framing, which is not only environmentally responsible, but also allows for greater design flexibility.

Commissioned by a Connecticut couple as a retirement home, the 5,500-square-foot home is built on 1.2 acres of riverfront property in Branford, Connecticut. From the very start, Sean Tracy and his colleagues, architects Todd Fouser and Rueben Jorsling of the Brooklyn-based firm FACE Design, viewed their first residential commission as an opportunity to test the firm's long held ideas about creating affordable yet imaginative residential architecture unrestrained by standard construction materials and methods.

For their part, the clients wanted a house that was low maintenance and able to withstand the vagaries of New England's seasonal changes. They also wanted a home that was modern but at the same time responsive to the unpretentious local vernacular architecture

LEFT: The distinctive sloping roofline created by a unique system of arched steel frames and innovative curved SIPs results in an airtight interior with expansive soaring spaces. The defunct shipyard buildings and old warehouses that populate New England's coastal towns inspired the utilitarian look of the galvanized steel-clad exterior.

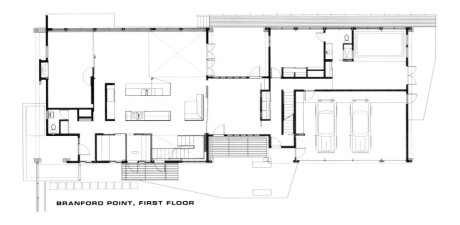

BRANFORD POINT, FIRST FLOOR

BRANFORD POINT, SECOND FLOOR

of barns, industrial warehouses, and dockyards surrounding the Connecticut landscape. Further, the house had to be private yet still allow the opportunity to engage with the heavy river traffic of pleasure boats and working vessels. Responding to the challenge, the team at FACE Design came up with the idea for a prefabricated kit of parts, consisting of pre-engineered

OPPOSITE: The light-filled lounge area of the second-floor mezzanine leads to the outdoor breezeway roof deck. The sizeable bridge-like platform spans the entire length of the second floor. The windows were computer analyzed to take advantage of the waterfront views and to maximize natural light and ventilation.

steel tube and arches, structural insulated panels, and glass panels. These versatile components proved light and flexible enough to incorporate a mass of seemingly contradictory needs of the clients into a vibrant yet cohesive building program.

The benefits of steel frame construction are immediately visible in the large volume of space present on the interior of the main house and its adjoining guest quarters. This is achieved by an inventive system of factory-made hollow steel-tube frames, comprising of thirteen arched ribs in all, which slope from the ceiling towards the ground. The ribs are bolted onto braces firmly anchored to the concrete foundation. To further strengthen the frame, horizontal I beams span across the arch frames and are connected at various points, forming a structurally tight self-supporting steel frame that dispenses with the need for load-bearing walls or structural columns. Just as innovative is the use of structural insulated panels (also known as SIPs), which consist of super insulated precut foam up to six inches thick, sandwiched between rectangular wood boards cut to industry-wide standard size. Reflecting the firm's inventive approach to problem solving, a company was hired to create prestressed curved structural insulated panels to accommodate the sloping parts of the roof. Noting his firm's collaborative approach, Tracy explained, "After interviewing a few leaders in the industry, the decision was made to work with Panel Pros out of New Hampshire because of their

enthusiastic approach and willingness to attempt new applications." The combination of a steel frame and nearly airtight, energy-efficient exterior skin sets the stage for the spatial gymnastics of Branford Point's dynamic interior.

The interior of the main house is defined by a dramatic mezzanine, which contains the sleeping areas and spans the length of the second floor, forming a bridge that overlooks the double-height great room and library space below. Strategically placed ribbon window strips run across the rear wall of the mezzanine, creating a light-filled area that almost appears to float above the interior. The "captain-of-the-ship" feel is reinforced by the mezzanine bridge, which provides commanding views of the river beyond and links indoor and outdoor spaces. The bridge

LEFT: The spacious open-plan interior is linked by subtle shades of gray. In keeping with the overall integrated design, the furniture, lighting, and shelving were all specially fabricated in the firm's workshop. ABOVE: The unobtrusive gray kitchen boasts a commanding central location between the living and dining areas.

analogy is both literal and figural, as the mezzanine mediates the transition from second level to the upper deck breezeway. A wood and glass stairway also links the second-floor mezzanine to the ground floor.

The open-plan ground floor contains a flexible living room that comes with a series of built-in steel and glass sliding walls that allow the space to be reconfigured. The kitchen, located under the mezzanine, is a central element that links the dining room, great room, and library—all with outside views—at one end of the house, and the pantry, office, and bath on the other side. The ground-floor breezeway connects the family house to the smaller guest wing, which contains the guest rooms, a spa, garage, and second-floor music studio.

Branford Point by all accounts is a success. Its owners, an active retired couple who spend a great deal of time at home, were pleased with the results and even the once-skeptical neighbors, who hoped for a more conservative salt box, have warmed to the house. For the architects at FACE Design, Branford Point served as a validation of their desire to find more integrated building process rather than the traditional architect-to-builder relationship. Producing the house was not too different from the way an airplane or car might be conceived and design tested. The house was subjected to digital analysis and the design enhanced to take advantage of maximum light during winter months, deflect the summer heat, and to frame picturesque river views while affording maximum privacy. As a full-service design/build studio, they were fully involved at every stage throughout the construction process. The architects made use of the metal manufacturing studio annexed to their offices, which allowed them to experiment with forms and produce a range of custom-designed components such as windows, doors, furniture, lighting, and stairs.

From the beginning, Branford Point, also known as Prototype I, was viewed less as a singular residential project and more like a new test aircraft or automobile. Branford Point served as the beta version, an experimental template against which later models would be revised. The current Connecticut house, at the client's request, came with such optional extras as thermal heating and a larger-than-normal square footage, which made for a more expensive home than initially anticipated. The architects feel, however, there is room to create a leaner version within the reach of the new homebuyers at $150 per square foot. To prove their point, a second version of the house (Prototype II), reduced to a more affordable 2,200 square feet of space with three bedrooms and two baths, is currently in the works.

Branford Point is about escaping the confines of architecture and instead engineering livable space using digital technology in a collaborative endeavor to create spontaneity and comfort. Offering a glimpse of the future, Branford Point has more in common with industrial design practices than the more organic sketch-to-model architectural process. ▥

OPPOSITE: Industrial in feel yet elegantly designed, the steel and glass staircase was prefabricated off-site and installed as a whole component. ABOVE: The small, enclosed second-floor bedrooms contrast with the open, large, airy public spaces. The strategic placement of the skylight and windows create well-modulated, even lighting.

LV house

ROCIO ROMERO

Some of the best design solutions emerge out of real life challenges and the LV House by Rocio Romero is no exception. The architect's parents, unwilling to spend the hundreds of thousands it would take to build an oceanfront vacation home in Laguna Verde, Chile, commissioned their daughter to come up with something more in line with their budget. After evaluating various options, the architect settled on a prefabricated kit of parts; a cost-effective, transportable dwelling that could be easily erected on top of scenic, rugged cliff-top terrain without the need for a lot of skilled labor. Romero came up with an open-plan, multiuse space optimally configured for living, sleeping, dining, and relaxation and christened it "LV," for Laguna Verde. The entire domestic program was inserted into a 1,150-square-foot rectangular envelope attractively clad in Galvalume. Rocio Romero's vacation home for her parents turned out to be an invaluable prototype that provided the architect a lesson in the art of combining low-cost, low-maintenance materials with high design.

The lessons of the LV House were equally applicable closer to home in the United States with a growing market of first-time homeowners and others looking for second homes as affordable vacation houses. Architectural photographer Jennifer Watson

OPPOSITE: Perched on the top of a hill surrounded by the Virginia Mountains, the wall of glass framing the front and side elevation provides panoramic views of the tree-filled landscape. ABOVE: The silvery Galvalume steel siding reflects the constantly shifting light patterns. In contrast to the open glass façade, the rear elevation is more reticent; smaller clerestory windows ensure privacy while allowing in light.

LV HOUSE, FIRST FLOOR

and her musician husband, Barry, had the honor of owning the first LV kit to roll off the production line in 2004, confirming Romero's instincts for her audience. The LV kit house is do-it-yourself friendly, although the architect strongly advises hiring a general contractor for a faster and more efficient building process. Jennifer and Barry Watson, in an effort to keep costs as low as possible, however, opted to go the do-it-yourself route, confident that his twenty-years construction experience as a renovations carpenter and her work as a surveyor and carpenter's helper would see them through. In addition, the Watsons had an impressive support system of family members in the construction business to draw on, not to mention a couple of University of Virginia architecture student volunteers.

Taking advantage of the LV's flexible design, owners Jennifer and Barry Watson were able to reconfigure

RIGHT: The compact open-plan living space is divided into sitting, dining, and kitchen areas. Clerestory windows located above the rear and side elevations ensure that light filters evenly throughout the house, including to the kitchen where the use of wall space for storage and plumbing prevents large picture windows.

the LV kit's standard two-bedroom, one bathroom interior, creating in addition to the standard main bedroom, a two-person shower and a multipurpose room for her children, complete with built-in storage areas. The compact 1,150-square-foot house, with its open-plan living, dining, and kitchen area never manages to feel constricted as a result of the LV House's pragmatic use of space. All the service areas, including the kitchen, bathrooms, utility, and media closets, are located towards the rear of the house. The LV's standard fixtures include stainless steel custom kitchen cabinetry, recessed dimmable lighting, and built-in speakers.

The Watson family rechristened their new LV home Luminhaus, in recognition of the natural light that filters through the home's generous sliding glass doors and windows. The expanse of glass also draws in the surrounding 6.2-acre property with its panoramic views of the Virginia mountains. The LV House's metal gray Galvalume exterior cladding reflects the changing shifts of light that occur throughout the day and the seasons beyond. The house's connection to nature— the architect's original design goal—is palpable. Visitors to Luminhaus, which is rented as a modern-style vacation getaway during months when it is unoccupied, can experience nature firsthand.

As sales volume increase, the LV should become more affordable. The basic kit costs $31,000. With shipping, construction fees, and optional extras factored in, the LV can cost anywhere between $86,000 and

$150,000. Equally important though, is the kit home's ability to provoke expressions of delight. As LV homeowner Jennifer Watson observed on seeing her house during a snowfall, "... absolutely beautiful." ■

OPPOSITE and ABOVE: Floor-to-ceiling windows and glass sliding doors frame the open-plan living/dining area as well as the enclosed bedroom, providing passive solar energy through natural sunlight. The generous picture windows also embrace the natural woodland scenery and views of the mountains beyond.

adriance house

ADAM KALKIN

Shock and awe is more than likely the general reaction to many a building by architect Adam Kalkin, and the Adriance House (also known as the 12 Container House), set in the bucolic coastal town of Brooklin, Maine, is no exception. Commissioned as a vacation home by advertising executive Anne Adriance and her business consultant husband, Matthew, Kalkin's container house initially met with much skepticism, if not disapproval from the community. Commenting in a *New York Times* article on reactions to the house, Anne Adriance philosophically explained, "It's so far outside of people's context for a 'house' that they don't have the emotional language to envision it. Their first reaction is curiosity and confusion."

Kalkin is a master at mining the materials of our industrial wasteland and reusing his finds in unexpected ways within a domestic context. As an artist, his modus operandi is to disrupt our tendency to intellectually and emotionally compartmentalize our reaction to public and private architecture. In our dulled domestic landscape the Adriance House calls

RIGHT: Double-height glass walls frame the front and back elevations and provide sweeping views of the trees and ocean beyond. The exuberant open central space contrasts with smaller, more introverted rooms symmetrically set into the distinctive orange container boxes on either side of the building.

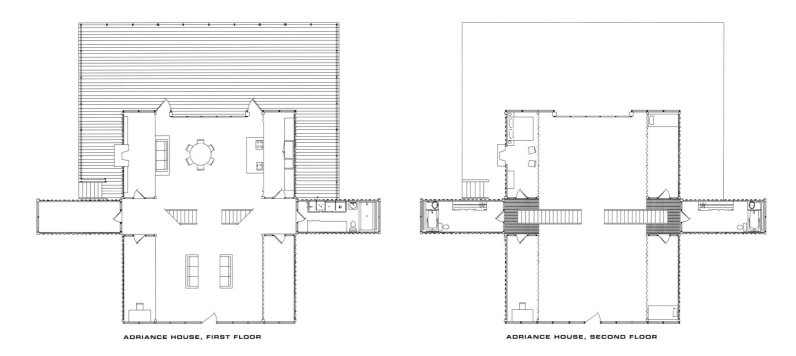

ADRIANCE HOUSE, FIRST FLOOR

ADRIANCE HOUSE, SECOND FLOOR

into question our dependence on historical domestic building conventions and traditions in deciding what is architecturally acceptable, especially where materials are concerned. Apart from shipping containers, other industrial materials used to great effect include scaffolding, concrete, corrugated metal, garage doors, and grating. The spatial gymnastics and formal dynamism

OPPOSITE: A distinctive, orange shipping container with stamped, striated patterns forms a cozy sitting room shell complete with a fireplace. A second-story container bedroom can be reached via a simple metal stairway. A rustic table in the dining area forms a counterpoint to the industrial feel of the setting.

of the airport jetway, warehouse, and loading dock are also used in Kalkin's souped-up domestic buildings. "Why not transfer the experiences associated with these industrial spaces into reimagining our domestic habitat?" Kalkin seems to be asking. The structural and environmental benefits of using recycled shipping containers aside, Kalkin appears to be addressing these unresolved questions in his domestic architecture.

For all the fuss that the 4,000-square-foot Adriance House seems to have initially engendered, there is something remarkably sedate about the end result. From the front elevation, the distinctive two-story orange cargo containers that form part of the residential wings are like visual ballasts that give a perfectly symmetrical balance and sense of solidity

to the house. The front and rear elevations are framed by a huge two-story curtain wall of glass, which not only invites sunlight but also draws in cooling summer breezes, providing more than adequate cross-ventilation. The sweeping front-to-back glass walls create generous Imax eye-views of the tree-filled landscape and stunning oceanfront scenery beyond. An elegant shallow pediment caps the front and rear elevation roofline in what seems to be a playful "lifeline" of normalcy, a concession of comforting domestic familiarity amid the unusual cargo container architecture. The bold, welcoming exterior is a dramatic opening chord that hints at the spatial drama inside.

The interior of Adriance House is defined by a huge double-height central open-plan space that forms the main public zone of the house, which includes a living room at one end and a dining area opposite. A double staircase placed to the left and right of the central space cleverly acts as a natural divider between the dining and living room areas, while also providing access to the bedroom and bathroom cargo modules above. The pair of staircases is rather long and narrow and set at a low, sloping angle. The feet of each staircase casually rest like a ladder against the cement floor. Wood steps provide a warm contrast to the cool metal balustrades and austere, rounded railings. The stairways seem to invite domestic flights of industrial fancy and look more like gangways rescued from a vintage jet airplane or defunct power station.

OPPOSITE: A container shell is used to create a ready-made enclosed kitchen space. A freestanding kitchen unit complete with built-in sink and ample space for working and casual dining extends the narrow kitchen area. ABOVE: A container bedroom located on the first floor is meticulously finished inside with cozy furnishing. Each container is framed by large picture windows, which make the cell-like rooms appear spacious while providing views of the outdoor scenery.

If the public areas of the house are defined by a soaring extroverted space, the private areas of the house are contained in a set of six, two-story-high cargo modules that flank either side of the great room and are arranged in a T-shape. The corrugated pattern of the containers and their distinctive orange color visually define the more private and introverted parts of the house. The second-floor cargo modules house bedrooms and bathrooms, and the first-floor container rooms house a kitchen, extra bedroom, and a small cozy book-lined living room complete with built-in fireplace. Each module is capped by floor-to-ceiling picture windows, which provide every room with ample light as well as a larger sense of space that embraces the wonderful views of the outdoors.

Available at a starting cost of $250,000 and more, depending on terrain and extras, the 12 Container House is a home on a grand scale. In spirit, it has something in common with the Great Camps of the Adirondacks, except instead of using felled logs to capture the theater of time and space, discarded container hulks are architecturally retrofitted as magnificent platforms for living and viewing nature. As architectural critic Alastair Gordon, writing in *The New York Times,* so aptly observed, "If every object has its day, then the steel shipping container may be the log cabin of the 21st century."

A much smaller, though no less imaginative, version of the 12 Container House can be purchased for considerably less money. The Quik House, as the

five-container kit's name implies, can be delivered anywhere in the continental United States relatively quickly within ten weeks of placing an order. Arriving on a flatbed truck, the kit of parts consists of five container shells, which can be joined together in as little as a week and completely finished inside and out within three months. The basic version of Quik House, which was exhibited at Dietch Gallery in New York,

OPPOSITE: An industrial-looking staircase leads to the second-floor container bedrooms and bathrooms. ABOVE LEFT: Bright white walls, curtains, and wood furniture enhance the cleverly converted bedroom container. A skylight invites additional daylight into the bedroom. ABOVE RIGHT: The second-story bathroom container is simple and practical and defined by a playful, attention-grabbing red waterproofed floor.

allows us to get a feel for the architect's sensibility. The carefully laid out 2,000-square-foot space is full of contrasts between open and closed areas, hard and plush textures, extroverted and private zones. The open-plan first-floor area places the living room right in the center of social activity of the house, adjacent to the kitchen and fireplace. Tucked off to the side are three enclosed areas. In the middle section is a cozy diner-style space, which serves as the dining room. On either side of the dining room is a pantry and closet/storage area. If the first floor serves as the more extroverted part of the house, the second floor is more complex with shifting levels of privacy. A compact staircase tucked off to the side leads to a second-floor study/living area, a semi-private space, which mediates between the more public and private spaces, including the master bedroom with en suite bath on one side of the house, and two additional bedrooms on the other side. In a deft touch, which playfully acknowledges the tight space, the additional bedrooms are furnished with

OPPOSITE, ABOVE and BELOW LEFT: The skillful linking of containers creates a carefully articulated interior built around a central open-plan living room and kitchen area. A compact cozy dining nook is tucked off to the side. **OPPOSITE, BELOW RIGHT:** The minimalist second-floor extra bedroom contains a space-saving steel bridge-style bed. A picture window illuminates the room and adds to the feeling of spaciousness.

"bridge beds" that are wedged head-to-toe between each end of the container. Without visible support, the beds appear to levitate. The touches reveal Kalkin's skill at enriching the domestic space with allusions to our industrial high-tech landscape; the minimalist bedrooms feel more like the luxe version of a sleeping area of a submarine or space station module bunk bed. Floor-to-ceiling windows cap each end of the second-floor container shell and allow plenty of light in each room.

The Quik House catalogue, downloadable from the architect's website, offers an array of options with a consumer friendliness that has more in common with buying a car or Dell or Apple computer than buying a house in the traditional sense. Among a long list of choices, you can select the style of windows you want or state your preference for turf or wood roof deck. You can even choose the color of the shipping containers, orange or natural "Rust Bloom," and for the environmentally committed the latest solar energy upgrades are available. The basic unfinished Quik House kit costs around $76,000 including shipping. The more luxurious Premium House Kit includes a whole array of finishes including mahogany sliding doors, two steel bridge beds, Maurer light fixtures, Iserman carpets, dining nook benches and table, as well as other components such as a fireplace and an HVAC package. The total cost of a fully furnished Quik house, depending on the model and optional extras, may cost anywhere between $150,000 and $175,000.

option house

BAUART ARCHITECTS

ABOVE: Large picture windows provide plenty of sunlight and generous views in two directions, giving the small house a feeling of spaciousness. OPPOSITE: The kit house comes complete with designer furniture. Inventive space-saving design includes a partition that serves double duty as a display wall in the living room and a storage cabinet in the kitchen area.

Simplicity, adaptability, comfort. These are the guiding principles at work in the design of Option House, which from a distance could easily be mistaken for a pristine sculpture installation by Donald Judd. Design and the appeal to the eye are completely inseparable from the practical aspects of the house. The house feels like the interior of a luxury yacht, where space is at a premium and has to be used artfully but judiciously. The house comes fully furnished with an elegant minimalist Philippe Starck bathtub and sink, a choice of "sky blue" glass or gray granite bathroom tile, as well as a suite of high-end brand-name furniture by the Bauhaus-inspired German company Hültsa. The interior furnishings consist of a sideboard, sofa, bookrack, bed, two cabinets, and two workbenches. As WeberHaus, the Swiss distributor of Option House, notes the house is "an ideal mix of high-tech combined with the desire for cocooning."

Ample light pours in from large double-glazed picture windows located on the second floor of the front elevation and the first floor of the rear elevation. Two more picture windows, one located on the second floor of the left-side elevation, and the other on the first floor of the right-side elevation form a playful geometrical pattern. The witty two-up, two-down window

kitchen and sitting room sections. In keeping with the rigorous pruning away of wasteful space, a large floor-to-ceiling dual-purpose cabinet serves both as a storage unit and partition separating the living room from the kitchen and dining areas. An elegant, unobtrusive wood staircase with glass side panels and a polished metal rail leads to the second-floor hallway, and in turn to the sole bedroom located at the front of the house. A bathroom and a small work area are located in the rear. Even the hallway serves an additional purpose with a built-in closet accessed by floor-to-ceiling mirrored folding doors.

True to its name, Option House is all about choice and the possibilities for expansion are endless. Should you feel the need for additional space, you can simply add another module and double your living room space. The extra module cleverly plugs into a side elevation wall to form an L-shaped plan. This is just the beginning, however, as the plug-in possibilities of modular design offer other combinations that can grow or shrink as the family changes. There is the "Two Option House" combination in which an additional twin module is added to the first one. An elegant glass atrium connects the two modules, so the whole construction forms a U-shape pattern. Multifamily expansion, from additional living or working quarters to a guesthouse, can be accommodated. Offering further expansion, two modules can become three, and can be staggered in a pattern reminiscent of Victorian terrace housing.

arrangement provides generous views that add to the feeling of spaciousness and also allows ample opportunity for cross ventilation and passive solar heating.

The two-story 750-square-foot house consists of an open-plan first-floor area divided into dining,

ABOVE: The bedroom is a minimal but enriched space enhanced by natural light that pours in from the picture window and by the comforting feel of wood flooring. OPPOSITE: Every inch of space engages the senses to the full. Compact, streamlined furniture, wood floors, and picture windows are all beautifully integrated into the living room.

Optional extras are available much in the way a carmaker might offer additional parts. There is a freestanding or connectable carport, a roof terrace addition, an awning, as well as a terrace, all of which can be had at extra cost. WeberHaus will also work with owners to alter certain elements to suit building codes and the environmental constraints of warm or cold climates.

The entire house is prefabricated off-site in a factory. Standardized precut timber forms the rectangular exterior frame and wood panels are then slotted in place. The exterior is finished with handsome wood strip siding. The interior is completely kitted out and then the entire structure is transported in two sections to its final destination, where it is set on existing footings or a foundation if more than one module is being used. Hooking up to water and electricity mains is the responsibility of the homeowner. In general, the whole setup can be made ready for occupation in as little as a day. Currently available only in Europe, Option House's one-bedroom, single-family unit costs 87,000 Euros, or $106,000 at today's rate.

Option House as a package challenges many assumptions we take for granted about modern living, chief among them is that small spaces are little better than leftovers and a pretext for sacrificing quality of life. As Bauart Architects set out to demonstrate in this intelligent approach to living, small spaces and comfortable surroundings need not be mutually exclusive ideals. ▥

loftcube

STUDIO AISSLINGER

The ultra-modern Loftcube is a unique rooftop kit home specifically designed for urban living in cramped cities. Its recommended mode of delivery, via helicopter, is eye-catching and rather glamorous, like the opening scene of a James Bond movie. One can almost imagine the clattering sound of a helicopter as it dangles the pristine white Loftcube over the city skyline, in time to the slick opening strains of the ubiquitous Bond theme music.

The Loftcube is designed to meet the challenges and constraints of rooftop spaces. The windy conditions of high-rise living are controlled using a variety of measures: Four weighted concrete pillars hold down the module, anchoring the Loftcube firmly to the ground and minimizing wind drag. The height of the module, raised four feet off the ground, also enhances the dwelling's wind-resistant aerodynamic quality. The combination of functionality and design is reflected in the Loftcube's handsome iPod-shaped curved exterior frame, which is not only structurally reinforced for added strength, but is stylish as well, giving the exterior

OPPOSITE: Minimizing the windy conditions of rooftop living, the Loftcube is lifted four feet off the ground by weighted feet, preventing the structure from being buffeted. The sleek rounded steel frame further enhances the wind-resistant aerodynamic quality of the Loftcube.

loftcube

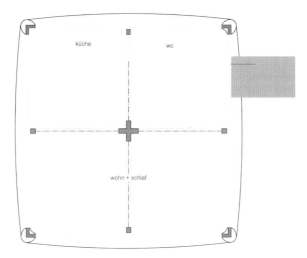

küche   wc

wohn + schlaf

LOFTCUBE, FIRST FLOOR

hygiene. The Loftcube is designed to be as functional and flexible as possible, the latest synthetic materials are used in innovative ways in order to achieve these goals. Movable partitions are created from double-sided "Glacier White" Dupont Corian panels, which are placed on tracks and glide back and forth, screening off the bath from the kitchen and living areas. With space at a premium, dual-purpose elements cleverly serve multiple parts of the compact interior. The bath area is adjacent to the kitchen and shares a tap that can be swiveled to serve either space and the shower-head, too, can be just as effortlessly swung around to water plants in the living room. The widespread use of durable, non-porous, and stain-resistant DuPont Corian in the kitchen, toilet, shower unit, and even for shelving, makes cleaning quick, easy, and efficient.

The integrated design philosophy at work in the Loftcube extends to matching furnishing, which is sold as a separate package. The portable modular furniture includes Werner Aisslinger's "Case" line, designed for the top furniture manufacturer Interlübke, as well as his famous "Gel" lounge chair in hot orange, designed for the equally illustrious modern furniture company Cappellini.

The Loftcube is shipped dismantled as a kit of parts in a 40-foot standard container. The "Basic" version costs $79,000 to $87,000 and consists of the outer shell and flooring—wall panels and internal plumbing are available as extras. A deluxe version, dubbed "Living," includes the Corian kitchen as well

a sleek look. The hollow metal of the exterior frame also provides channels for wiring. Sheets of acrylic glass frame the exterior façade of the module and an extra covering of laminated wood louver windows provide protection from the glare of sunlight, inevitable in high-rise living. Customers may choose from a mix of clear, matte, and colored glass tinted orange, brown, or light blue according to the degree of privacy desired.

The compact 387-square-foot open-plan interior contains distinct zones for living, sleeping, and

OPPOSITE: The open-plan interior is loosely divided into distinct zones for sleeping, living, hygiene, and cooking. Compact modular furniture is flexible and can be arranged to suit various needs. Translucent acrylic sliding glass outer panels reduce the glare of the sunlight.

as a toilet and shower unit and costs between $93,000 and $99,000. The kit is put together on the ground and then the completed 2.5-ton module is hoisted by freight helicopter, or height permitting by construction crane, to its rooftop site.

With acres of unused car park, apartment, and townhouse rooftops in major cities throughout the world, Aisslinger sees a financial incentive for landlords, tenants, or building management to rent or own rooftop dwellings. If nothing else, the Loftcube challenges city planners and dwellers alike to imagine a new way of living in order to alleviate our overcrowded cities. ▪

OPPOSITE: Double-sided Corian panels serve as movable partitions, sliding back and forth to provide privacy as needed. Floor surfaces emphasize various functions: Carpeting is used for sleeping and living areas, Dupont Zodiaq, a quartz-based material, is used for the kitchen, and white-washed gravel covers the bathroom floor. ABOVE LEFT: The smooth, rounded edge of the Corian sink is echoed in the overall design. ABOVE RIGHT: A simple, elegant column of Corian serves as the shower.

now**house**

T O B Y   L O N G   D E S I G N

ABOVE: The elegant two-tone exterior is clad with aluminum sheets and recycled wood, punctuated by carefully placed windows, which provide adequate natural light while providing privacy. OPPOSITE: The NowHouse's energy-efficient structural insulated panel framing system enables the large, open-plan double-height space, which defines the living room.

Eco-friendly, high tech, and flexibly designed to manage a lifetime of change, the NowHouse is a 21st-century model for sustainable living.

Although the NowHouse is designed to fit in with a diverse range of locations and domestic living arrangements, in many ways, the 2,400-square-foot prefabricated dwelling is a new and improved update of a classic suburban home. Its sober two-tone exterior siding is distinctive but not over-the-top. Measured, pragmatic, and unlike most conventional housing, the NowHouse provides for future growth through customizable and expandable interiors; everything about the design is carefully calibrated to make the most of the challenges and constraints of modern life.

At the heart the NowHouse's recipe for modern living is an easy-to-assemble and well-planned building system comprised of a kit of parts made up of pre-engineered wall and roof structural insulated panels (SIPs). With the ability to withstand winds of 160 miles per hour the SIPs' load-bearing capacity is evenly dispersed throughout the exterior walls, getting rid of the need for internal supporting walls, allowing for a great deal of flexibility in arranging the floor plan.

The first floor has an airy open-plan design with distinct public and private zones. On one side is

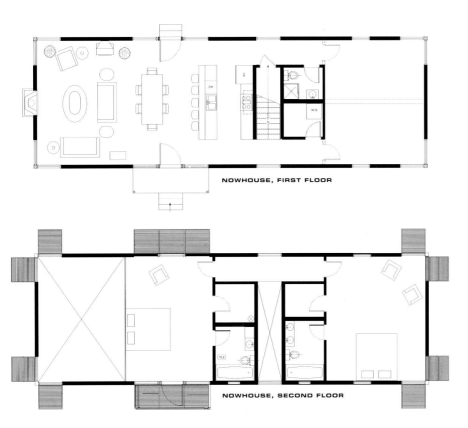

NOWHOUSE, FIRST FLOOR

NOWHOUSE, SECOND FLOOR

an open living, dining, and kitchen area divided by a bathroom and laundry, which acts as a buffer zone between the public and private halves of the house. The flow of space is very well thought out and leaves room for flexible arrangements in which the first-floor bedroom/office can be split in two. Doors placed on either side of the space anticipate separate

RIGHT: The elegant, welcoming, open-plan interior is separated into distinct cooking, dining, and living room areas. Stylish, modern furniture defines each separate area and the rich, dark finish of the wood visually links the whole space. Floor-to-ceiling vertically arranged windows fill the house with natural light. A second-floor loft space overlooks the double-height living area below.

kit homes modern

entrances for newly created rooms. The second floor consists of a master bedroom with an en suite bathroom and an additional loft-style room, which may be used as a junior bedroom or family room.

Flexibility is a key part of the NowHouse. As the company brochure emphasizes, "By adding simple interior partitions, the house can accommodate from two to five bedrooms. We can also change the overall dimensions of the building to provide for any site constraints or permit regulations, or to provide for additional space." In its forward-thinking, flexible program, the NowHouse places the sustainability of family life on the same footing as its energy-conservation agenda. The former, often ignored by the homebuilding industry, is arguably just as important. According to a recent *Better Homes and Gardens* magazine survey of 60,000 respondents, "people currently only stay in a home for three to five years due to expanding family." The house is pre-engineered to grow according to an owner's needs and budget. The NowHouse can start out as a one-story dwelling, and as the family grows, a second floor can be added using a unique system of detachable roof and wall sections. Additional features such as a roof deck, stand-alone garage, or carport can be added as the need arises. NowHouse is available for around $150 per square foot. An upgraded kit, complete with optional interior finishes such as bamboo cabinets, KitchenAid appliances, and other accessories is available for about $200 per square foot. ▥

OPPOSITE: The more private second-floor family loft room is less formal and overlooks the double-height living room below. Natural light is beautifully orchestrated and filters in from all angles. Clerestory awning windows allow excess heat to escape and enable daylight to illuminate the loft. ABOVE: Eco-friendly new-growth bamboo flooring is used in the bedroom and throughout the house.

flatpak **house**

LAZOR OFFICE

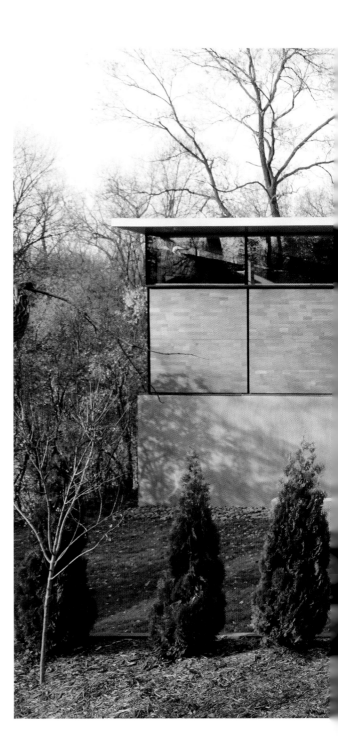

With the visual panache that might accompany the brochure for a car or computer, the catalogue for the Flatpak House features an array of options and elegant finishes that entices the reader with endless possibilities.

With its unpretentious materials, harmonious design, and flexible layout, the Flatpak offers a vision of modern living with which few might find hard to disagree. The house is the brainchild of Charlie Lazor, a co-founder of BLU DOT furniture design company, noted for its use of innovative materials and fabrication technology to produce elegant and affordably priced furniture. Lazor, a critic of the lack of choice and slow response of the mainstream construction industry to developing quality modern housing, set out to prove that affordability and quality are not mutually exclusive ideals. "Architecture for the ordinary pocket book" was a guiding principle for Lazor and his aim from the outset was to bring the same rigor and detail normally given to custom design within the reach of the average home owner. With these goals in mind, the Lazor Office was formed in 2003 to realize his goal of quality affordable modern houses.

RIGHT: The elegant Flatpak design is made up of a flexible kit of parts, which includes eight-foot cement sections, wood panels, and large picture windows. The second-floor translucent walkway covers the courtyard, linking the family and guest quarters.

flatpak house

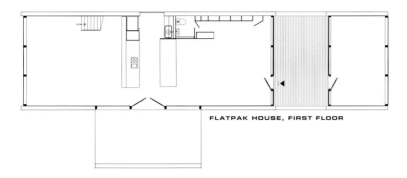

FLATPAK HOUSE, FIRST FLOOR

FLATPAK HOUSE, SECOND FLOOR

To make the Flatpak House affordable yet flexible enough to accommodate a variety of floor plans, Lazor decided on a system of prefabrication based for the most part on standardized interchangeable components. Finding little enthusiasm for the Flatpak concept from more traditionally minded prefab manufacturers, Lazor, with an eye on quality and consistency, sourced materials from a variety of suppliers, not unlike the way the advanced car or airplane maker might outsource components often made off-site by specialists and then transported and assembled at the factory. Similarly the components of the Flatpak House, from the standardized eight-foot wood panels to sheet glass, are manufactured by specialist suppliers and then assembled and trucked to the site.

The first Flatpak House, numbered "001" in the catalogue, was completed in the summer of 2004. Lazor and his family quite appropriately tested this first prototype. The streamlined kit of parts included concrete panels, metal-framed glass sheets, wood panels, and metal structural insulated panels for the roof. The 2,600-square-foot house took six months to build and began with the arrival of flatbed trucks bearing

the house's unique building system. The concrete foundation consisting of insulated concrete panels came precut complete with holes for stud walls and was put in place in a matter of days. On top of the concrete wall, a series of Douglas fir exterior panels are placed and capped by a slim band of windows that allow in light. These panels also provide maximum privacy on the more heavily trafficked west side of the house, which is located next to the popular Kenilworth Trail in Minneapolis. The opposite side of the house is more open, with floor-to-ceiling windows, which invite in the surrounding greenery. The streamlined horizontal façade of wood and glass is broken up by a covered thruway, which serves as a courtyard patio and dual entrance between the annexed study and the main house. The 20-by-70-foot house is capped by a

OPPOSITE: Contrary to the reputation prefabs have for careless construction, the exterior detail reveals the care and precision with which the intersecting components, such as wood panels and large picture windows, are meticulously joined.

well-insulated energy-efficient metal roof, which more than surpasses the Minnesota energy code.

The well-thought-out modern interior of the Flatpak is defined by a generous open-plan first-floor interior configured to suit Lazor and his family. The kitchen is centrally located between the living and dining areas, which at first Lazor's wife thought was odd, but later acknowledged in a *Minneapolis-St. Paul Star Tribune* article, "it really works for the way we live. We'll be right there with our kids." Upstairs on the second floor the master bedroom with bath is placed at one end of the house. In between the master bedroom and children's bedrooms is a play area. A walkway linking the main house to the guest quarters allows visitors some independence from the family.

As any true disciple of modern architecture will tell you, the devil is in the details, and Lazor, reinforced by his design background, has managed to incorporate an impressive array of large and small elements that work as a unifying whole, dispeling the stereotype of rickety prefabricated housing. The attention to detail reflected in the Flatpak certainly puts to shame the cookie-cutter Sheetrock camouflage aesthetic of comparably priced conventionally built housing. The detailing in the Flatpak House is both aesthetically pleasing and practical: Wood panels are designed to

RIGHT: In contrast to the reticent façade, the courtyard patio, located in between the glass-walled dining room and office/retreat, provides a transition between indoor and outdoor spaces. The second-floor walkway just above also provides an opportunity to observe or interact with the courtyard traffic below.

open in strategic places to allow cross ventilation, the concrete is carefully mixed to give it a smooth finish, and the interior and exterior panels are carefully joined to form as visually clean and pristine a look as possible. The interior walls are made of strengthened fiberboard coated with easy-to-clean epoxy paint. Kitchen countertops are elegant and inexpensively created using galvanized metal over plywood. Even the lighting is fully integrated into the overall design using specially created light curtains by noted designer Pablo Pardo. Care is taken as well with the look and feel of the kitchen and bathroom fixtures. Flatpak comes with sleek KitchenAid appliances selected from the company's appropriately titled "Architect Series" line, which Lazor also designed in collaboration with the creative team at KitchenAid. The bathroom fixtures are a global amalgam of stylish high-end parts from the German company Duravit and the equally stylish American bathroom fixtures firm Toto, among others.

One of the most interesting aspects of the Flatpak House is Lazor's realignment of the relationship between architect and client. It is true that conventional stick-built kit houses have traditionally allowed for more client input than usual, giving homeowners the opportunity to custom design their own houses, but that has always been a daunting option that all but the most intrepid do-it-yourselfers have embarked upon. With Flatpak, the flexible and interchangeable nature of its panelized building system lends a "plug-in" aspect to customizing your house,

making it potentially an altogether easier experience to contemplate. With the Flatpak system, Lazor, as architect, neatly avoids having already predesigned and preselected the architectural hardware. Lazor's role is more like that of a fellow collaborator, as he hands a flexible kit of parts for the consumer to use as he or she sees fit. Like a set menu with many items, the buyer can choose from a selection of four floor plans ranging from 1,600 to 2,600 square feet. There is also a choice of concrete, wood, cement board, metal, clear, or sandblasted glass exterior panels, all are available in a range of colors including a funky playful Madras plaid panel. Each material can be mixed and matched in an endless variety of combinations, lending degrees of privacy, openness, and expressiveness to the house. Among the flooring options are Douglas fir, birch veneer panels, concrete in light black, gray, and white, light blue epoxy, cork, environmentally friendly bamboo, or FLOR modular carpeting. With an embarrassment of riches, the homeowner gets to "art direct" the exterior and interior of the house, giving it his or her personal stamp. Depending on the site and choice of extras, the Flatpak House may cost anywhere from $190 to $200 per square foot. ▪

OPPOSITE: Floor-to-ceiling picture windows allow plenty of sunlight and overlook the more private side of the house.

the garden escape

With the population of people now working from home in the millions, and with even more expected to join the home business workforce, the home office, much in the way the eat-in kitchen defined the 20th-century home, is fast becoming the 21st century's latest contribution to the domestic sphere. Yet for many, the growing need for home workspace is not all that easy or cost-effective to realize. Building an annex to an existing house or redesigning set interiors to create extra space is costly, very often requiring not only the services of an architect and structural engineer but also the added headache of securing planning permission. Enter British entrepreneurs Richard and Kathleen Harvey and Matthew Gill, who, in the hope of attracting the UK's growing ranks of home office workers, have come up with the idea for a simple, cost-effective stand-alone dubbed "The Garden Escape." The business partners engaged the British design firm Metropolis Architecture to give shape to their idea for an upmarket shed.

Space and light are key elements in the Garden Escape's well-crafted one-room structure, with simple

RIGHT: Clad in western red cedar, this cozy garden office features a clean, contemporary look and compact size that creates a warm, welcoming environment designed to blend in with most garden settings. The wood-framed glass façade is double glazed and specially coated to reduce heat build up and glare.

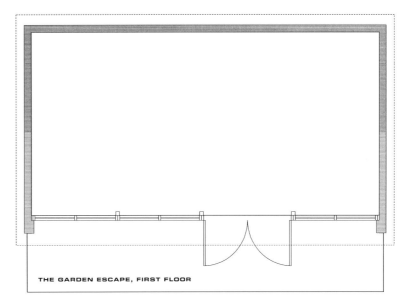

elegant lines enhanced by its handsome western red cedar wood exterior, which can be preserved and stained to your liking. The super shed is capped by an all-season, tilt-up roof. The front elevation is framed by generous floor-to-ceiling expanse of double-glazed doors and windows that flood the room with natural light, allowing the outside world in. The floors, walls, and windows of the year-round workspace is well insulated, some thirty to forty percent better than most homes, the maker's claim. The modern interior space is simple, with pristine white painted walls and an all-purpose laminated wood floor. Speed and simplicity is a marketing point: Without the need for planning permission in most cases, and with all but a

LEFT: The multi-purpose, flexible, open-plan space is carefully proportioned to human scale. The elegant wood trim and streamlined designer office furniture creates an aesthetically pleasing environment.

ABOVE: Conceived as a relaxing garden office or retreat, the elegantly designed shed works best in a setting where nature is a part of the overall design scheme. OPPOSITE: Light streams in from the open wood-framed sliding doors, which creates a welcoming informality, blurring the boundaries between workspace and garden.

basic foundation of 6 to 12 concrete piles required, the Garden Escape can be ready in as few as four to five days.

The interior of the Garden Escape office is as well appointed as any corporate suite. Electricity is drawn from the main building and powers office equipment, mounted spotlights, a convector heater, and multiple power points. Plumbing can also be installed by linking the structure with water utilities from the main house. Interior design services are available as a separate package, and include elegant Italian designer office furniture.

The meticulous construction of the Garden Escape's kit of parts is impressive. The precision-cut exterior wood strips and laminated floor planks, the perfect joinery of the window frames, and even the brass hooks that keep doors from slamming in the summer breeze are all finished with great attention to detail. This is no ordinary shack, but an elegantly conceived office setting that celebrates nature as much as it creates a positive environment of work.

Flexibility is an important selling point of the Garden Escape and the modular timber construction system allows great design variety and scope. The majority of requests are for office space. As the Garden Escape's Richard Harvey notes, "the benefits of having somewhere separate in which to concentrate during the day, but lock the door on at night are immense." Apart from office space, the stand-alone addition can also be adapted to suit a wide variety of purposes including a gym, a children's playroom, a teenage space, a sauna, or a yoga meditation space. A family of musicians with a house that was too small to accommodate everyone's music practice decided to turn their Garden Escape into a space for music jam sessions. Their Garden Escape music room was custom designed with such extras as triple glazing and walls inlaid with acoustic foam to enhance sound quality. The company prides itself on its flexibility and will assist in modifying the interior to suit the structure's use. The Garden Escape range comes in standard sizes designed to fit in a wide variety of garden spaces and outdoor situations. The comprehensive range of sizes includes 103-, 110-, 187-, 224-, 248-, and 294-square-foot spaces. If none of the standard sizes are suitable, the company will work with the buyer to create a custom-designed space. A new line called the Garden Escape Cube introduces a more compact minimal space for smaller garden settings. The basic 168-square-foot turnkey-ready Garden Escape, including interior decoration, lighting, telephone sockets, and power points, costs around $31,515.

With the population now working from home reaching 18 million, according to the United States Bureau of Labor Statistics, and with even more people expected to join the home business workforce, the home office is destined to become a permanent fixture in today's domestic space. Although the Garden Escape is not yet available outside of England, it is possible that it could just as easily be packaged and shipped in a container just about anywhere in the world. ▪

iT house

TAALMAN KOCH ARCHITECTURE

Individuality, choice, and the benefits of mass customization are all part of the equation of the iT House, which feels a bit like an architectural version of a beautifully designed Swatch Watch. The colorful, wraparound glass walls challenges the familiar stereotype of prefab architecture as nothing more than a patchwork of mundane cardboard-like materials. There is a sense of joy in the Starburst candy–like colors, which weave through the transparent glass skin of this customizable prefab kit.

The kit of parts is assembled from readily available off-the-shelf items, which include high-grade Bosch aluminum frames that arrive precut, predrilled, and ready for assembly, insulated double-glazed sheets of glass, insulated steel plank roofing, a freestanding Bulthaup Kitchen Workbench, complete with sink and tap fixtures, and plywood flat-pak cabinets with laminate surfaces. The kit also includes the iT House's signature transparent vinyl "outFits," which are bonded onto the sliding glass doors and windows, giving the house its unique decorative design. The "outFits," as

RIGHT: The lightweight, extra-strong Bosch aluminum frame supports floor-to-ceiling glass walls. Buyers can choose from a wide selection of custom-designed vinyl sheets, which are then fused onto the glass wall, providing an elegant colorful screen. The whole structure rests on a radiant-heat Smart Slab and is capped by an insulated steel roof.

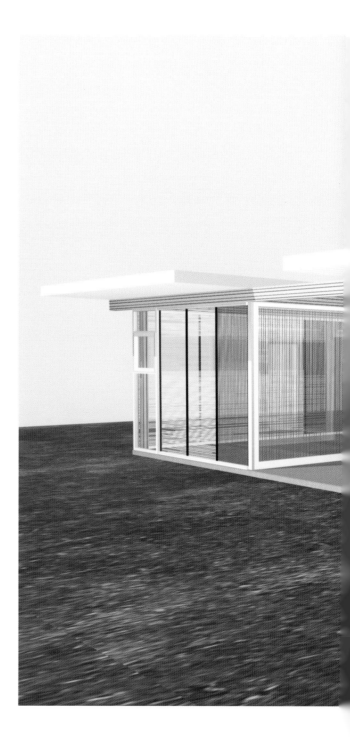

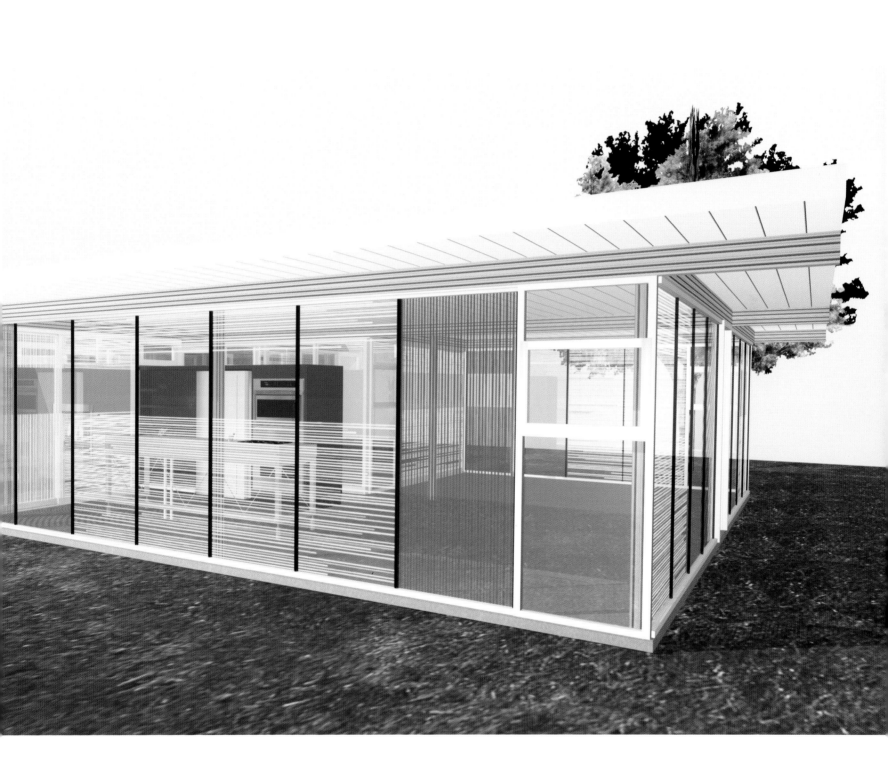

they are dubbed by Taalman Koch Architecture, are selected from a wide-ranging catalogue of specially commissioned designs. The iT House can be constructed in eight weeks and costs $175,000.

The entire structure rests on a 50-by-30-foot Smart Slab, which essentially functions as the life support system of the iT House. Embedded in the slab is a radiant heating system that efficiently and comfortably heats the house on cold days and also supports air-conditioning and electrical systems that assist in climate control and energy output.

The Bosch aluminum skeletal frame, on which the decorative glass panels are hung, has built-in channels and tracks for electrical wiring and add-on attachments such as curtains and shelving. The aluminum frame is exceptionally strong and is engineered to comply with California's tough seismic codes.

The 1,000-square-foot space is divided into public and private zones. One side contains a large master bedroom, a smaller adjacent room, which can be used as a bedroom or office, and the house's sole full bathroom. Two intimate courtyards, placed on opposite sides of the house, act as intermediary spaces between indoor and outdoor areas and private and public parts of the house. Entry and exit points are well thought out; despite the iT House's compact size, simultaneous public or private activities can be carried out without necessarily impinging on each other. Internal access to the rooms is organized around a central corridor, which feeds entry and exit

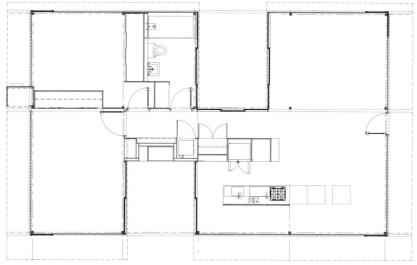

IT HOUSE, FIRST FLOOR

to both pubic and private spaces. In many ways this is a very social house that encourages a continuing conversation between indoor and outdoor areas; the courtyard's sliding doors provide entry to the living room and kitchen areas from the outside. The outdoor room with its fireplace would make a wonderful place for entertaining on cool summer evenings—its pragmatic siting adjacent to the kitchen allows food to be efficiently ferried back and forth. ▪

OPPOSITE: The all-glass house embraces nature and provides panoramic views in all directions. ABOVE: Two outdoor courtyards—one of which has a fireplace—blurs the boundary between indoor and outdoor spaces and encourages maximum social interaction.

modular 1 house

In a scene that might not look out of place in an aircraft or automobile factory where modular methods are routinely used, the Modular 1 House gives new meaning to the term a "kit of parts." Five 12-by-20-foot sections, which make up the 1,200-square-foot home, are rolled off the factory floor onto semitrucks and transported to their final destination; a deceptively easy "plug and play" image that never quite loses its power to impress.

Although the Modular 1 House was created as a one-off prototype home, it provides an excellent textbook example of how modular construction techniques are changing the way we think of the modern kit house as a packaged building system. The house, located in Kansas City, is not, however, merely a lesson in the latest advances in construction. More importantly, in an age in which prefabrication all too often stands for mass-produced standardization, Modular 1 House is a restatement of the central role of design and craftsmanship in creating affordable livable environments. The house is also about working

RIGHT: The reticent rectangular exterior is made warmer and more expressive by the use of massaranduba, a durable reddish brown Brazilian hardwood. A large floor-to-ceiling polycarbonate translucent picture window facing the street, filtering natural light through to the study while providing privacy.

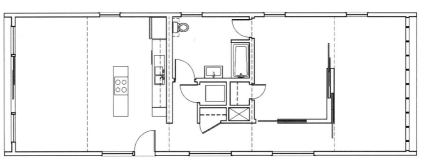

imaginatively within the limited rectangular framework of prefabricated modular construction methods.

Studio 804, the architectural collective behind the Modular 1 House, is made up of graduate students from the Kansas University School of Architecture and Urban Design. The school is highly regarded for its challenging project-based educational program. Over the years, Studio 804 projects, headed by Dan Rockhill, a highly respected architect and professor at Kansas University, have received numerous national and international awards.

The rather reticent exterior façade is elegantly framed by linear siding strips made from a handsome reddish-brown Brazilian hardwood called massaranduba, chosen by the collective for its eco-friendly and hardy attributes. The Sierra Club and the Forest Stewardship Council have both endorsed the responsible use of massaranduba. The Brazilian hardwood is tough and resistant to damage and is a Class A fire-resistant material similar to concrete and steel. The siding strips, attached to 1-by-2-foot boards cover the entire surface of the exterior, relieved only by

LEFT: The rectangular envelope contains a flexible open-plan living, dining, and kitchen space. Environmentally friendly bamboo wood flooring provides warmth and the sensuous feel of natural material. Large picture windows punctuate the side elevations, providing additional natural light.

windows that punctuate the side elevations. These large floor-to-ceiling translucent picture windows frame the front and rear façade and filter light into the interior. Aesthetic elements like the wood siding subtly serve as camouflage, hiding the utilitarian inner workings of the house such as gutters and a waterproof rubber layer that covers the roof and walls.

The interior is made up of six 200-square-foot self-contained modules, each with specific functions. Although designed as separate units, they are interchangeable and can be joined together to suit individual needs. The separate units come together to form a seamless whole: The living/dining area is joined to the kitchen area, together forming an open-plan space. The more private zones of the house are demarcated by a wall that separates the kitchen/living room from the bathroom bedroom and study. A corridor running the length of the house provides access to all the different parts. The organic, natural feel of the house is underscored by the use of sustainable materials such as the vertical-grain bamboo flooring, which runs the length of the house. Making the most of the limited space, the architects have managed to carve out 40 feet of shelving space.

Although the Modular 1 House was built as a prototype in partnership with City Vision Ministries and the Rosedale Development Association, two Kansas City nonprofit organizations that funded the project to the tune of $105,000, the market rate for a similar design would be in the range of $150,000. ▦

OPPOSITE: The main corridor runs the length of the house, linking the bedrooms, study, living area, bathroom, and kitchen. Built-in sliding-door partitions separate the bedroom from the common areas. ABOVE: The easy industrial-looking stainless steel bathroom walls contrasts with the light, open spaces in the rest of the house.

camp smull

Setting new standards for modular housing, architects Joseph Tanney and Robert Luntz, co-founders of the innovative New York firm Resolution: 4 Architecture, have created a unique mass-customized design system that consists of a catalogue of flexible rectangular forms, called the Bar System, that enables each prefab home to be put together in an infinite variety of ways. The results are not unlike the compositions of Philip Glass, whose spare musical notations create endless patterns of possibility despite the inherent limitations of his craft.

Tanney and Luntz's compositional fluency with rectangular forms was honed well over fifteen years ago in their thriving architectural practice, which specialized in the renovation of New York City lofts. The exorbitant cost of these loft apartments often required the rigorous analysis of every precious square foot of space to ensure their meaningful use. Working from the inside out, the architects developed a TV-like "picture-in-picture" proficiency in their ability to work the confines of compact, box-like spaces, turning them into more coherent and seamless modern interiors.

Although the architects have designed many distinguished lofts and conventionally built high-end modern homes, they have always had a long-standing interest in creating well-designed affordable prefab housing. Aware of the high failure rate of previous architects who tried their hand at manufacturing modern prefabs, Tanney and Luntz, after much study, came to the conclusion that they would not try to reinvent the wheel, but would work within the existing framework of the burgeoning, though somewhat conservative, prefabricated modular house manufacturing industry. The advantages of factory-built housing included a reduction in the amount of skilled on-site labor needed, since most of the construction takes place off-site at the factory. The ability to control costs has meant that the firm can offer prefabricated houses as meticulously created as their traditional $350-plus-per-square-foot stick-built custom designs, but at a more affordable cost of about $175 to $275 per square foot. While this price is still not cheap, the

OPPOSITE: The handsome cedar clad exterior of Camp Smull blends in with the surrounding woodland. The reticent placement of horizontal bands of windows preserves privacy on the more public side of the house. Building anticipation of the commanding view of the creek that awaits, a pathway leads from the rear main entry towards the inland waterfront scenery at the front of the house.

camp smull

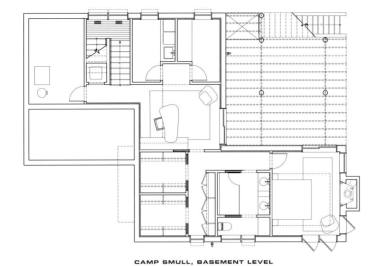

CAMP SMULL, BASEMENT LEVEL

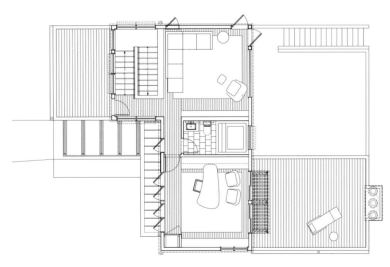

CAMP SMULL, FIRST FLOOR

CAMP SMULL, SECOND FLOOR

architects believe that with increasing volume the average cost of their modular modern homes may begin to decrease in the near future.

Resolution: 4 Architecture's growing library of rectangular bars reflects their commitment to modular construction methods, achieving a delicate balance between standardization and providing mass-customizable individual details. The ease with which a large degree of individualization can be built into their designs, not to mention the speed of executing the conceptual design phase, is in no small measure due to the clever mutations of rectangular modules, which form a flexible and responsive design framework. In an effort to streamline the design process, they have defined six primary modular styles: Single Bar, L-Series, Double-Wide, T-Series, Triple-Wide, and Z-Series. Each style has a subset of variations, called bars, that approximate actual modules that can be mixed and matched with other styles in the series.

Camp Smull, a 2,500-square-foot, three-level home located on the banks of the Harness Creek in Annapolis, Maryland, is defined by its orientation to the small but scenic plot set on less than an acre of land. Commissioned by Michael Smull, an education consultant, and his wife, Andy, a professional photographer, the house is based on Tanney and Lunz's "Z-Series" modular typology, which fits the narrow, sloping shape of the land and promotes a direct view of the creek. The exterior walls of the house are clad in wood, which fits in well with the natural environment and gives the impression of a house that sits in harmony with the land despite its small plot. The front elevation is punctuated by a combination of sliding doors, picture windows, and smaller clerestory windows, which flood the house with light in a carefully controlled way. The side and rear elevations, more open to public view, have smaller window openings that are set higher up to preserve privacy while also allowing light indoors.

The view of the creek and the surrounding woodland is given top billing: The first floor, set on the upper ground of the site's elevated, sloping terrain, contains an open-plan living, dining, and kitchen area as well as a generous deck—all overlooking the creek. The compact plan sandwiches the public areas of the house on the first floor between the more private self-contained areas on the second floor and a subterranean walk-out basement level. The subterranean master bedroom suite occupies an unusual space tucked into a sloping site. The walk-out basement contains the suite's sitting and sleeping areas, and has ample light, views of the water, and access to the creek via glass sliding doors. The rear part of bedroom suite, following the sloping gradient of the land, is more sheltered below ground and contains the more private service areas such as the bathroom and dressing room. A nocturnal logic places non-active nighttime functions lower down in the basement while more active events such as eating, working, entertaining, and engaging the scenery outdoors are located on the upper floors. Above the

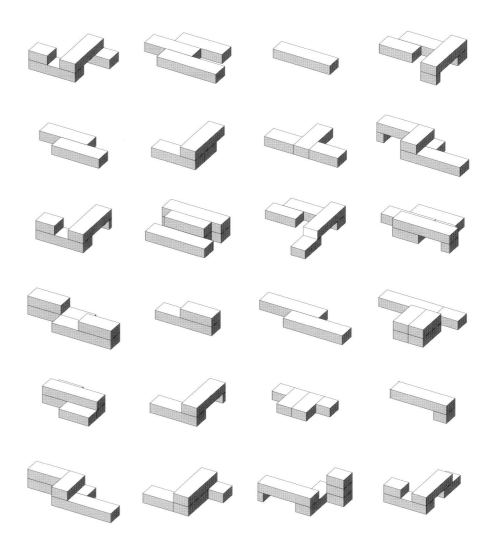

ABOVE: Variations on Resolution: 4 Architecture's unique modular housing types form a ready-made design system. The predesigned Bar System is highly flexible and responsive to the environmental conditions of a given site or a client's various needs.

basement-level master bedroom, the first-floor's welcoming open-plan public area invites the scenery indoors and provides a warm social space. An exterior staircase connected to the first-floor deck provides visitors independent access to the house from the dock. Tucked away on the cozy, tree house–like second floor are his and her studio workspaces. The self-contained second story has its own bathroom and the space could easily double as inviting guest quarters. Each studio opens out onto its own deck, providing even more commanding views of the surrounding landscape.

Among the houses that reveal the flexibility of Tanney and Luntz's bar system is Mountain Retreat, a 1,800-square-foot vacation home in Kerhonksen, New York. An adaptation of the Single Bar family of forms, the house is a combination of a Lifted Bar with a Two Story Bar, subsets of the Single Bar series. The result is an informal home suited to the owner's love of entertaining. The horizontal upper level with its generous living area and deck forms the perfect indoor/outdoor platform for viewing nature and casual social activities.

Hawk Ridge Residence, a 2,600-square-foot home in Ellenville, New York, offers yet another variation on the Single Bar theme. The familiar elongated horizontal bar used in the Mountain Retreat also favors the site's wide panoramic open views, though here the internal dynamics are quite different. Perched close to the edge of a ridge, the horizontal bar is completely opened up to create an exuberant welcoming response to the generous mountain views directly in front of the house.

The complex simplicity of the modular bar system can also be seen at work in plans for a Fire Island beachfront property just off Long Island, New York. Here the 3,400-square-foot home is defined by the narrow confines of the land: The substantial dwelling is elegantly stretched out in a multi-layered, attenuated horizontal bar, like the graceful bulk of an ocean liner. The three-bedroom, one-and-a-half-bathroom main house is detached from the guest quarters located towards the rear. An expansive upper deck, like an elevated pier, extends from the main house across to the three-bedroom, one-and-a-half-bath guest wing, forming a bridge that unites the two structures. At considerably less cost than a more labor-intensive on-site building, the Fire Island house was constructed off-site in a factory, shipped by barge to its final location, and then hoisted into place by a crane—a process that not only would have taken much longer and cost more using traditional construction methods, but also minimized disruption to the immediate environment.

With its unique modular design system, Resolution: 4 Architecture has pushed the envelope of prefab residential architecture quite far, streamlining if not "prefabricating," the design process itself. The rich array of precast forms helpfully translates the architect's concepts, which are clearly laid out for the client or layman, not unlike an upscale, meticulously designed version of a sushi photo ID menu. ▪

OPPOSITE TOP and **BOTTOM** and **ABOVE**: Mountain Retreat, Kerhonksen, New York (top). Hawk Ridge Residence, Ellenville, New York (bottom). Beach House, Fire Island, New York (above). Despite the limits of the basic modular rectangular shell, these renderings reveal the possibilities of mass customization using various materials and in the massing of rectangular volumes.

bale classic cabin

In many ways the TomaHouse Bale Classic Cabin transcends time and space. It represents the kind of global partnership and enterprise that may well point the way to the house of the future. The mini dwelling was conceived by a German entrepreneur, its frame engineered by an aerospace scientist who once worked for NASA, and its traditional design created by an Australia-trained architect based in Bali with input from a famous Indonesian master schooled in the ancient art of feng shui.

The best inventions are often born out of necessity and the Bale Classic Cabin is no exception. Economist and entrepreneur Frank Thoma wanted a small, affordable, self-contained home with high aesthetic values that could also be quickly erected. He was drawn to the possibilities of prefabricated housing but became disappointed by what he found.

OPPOSITE: Though the bedroom module is traditional in design, the classical, simple lines of the Indonesian-style timber panels resonate with an understated modernist aesthetic. The raised platform patio creates a distinct space separating the outdoors from the luxurious indoor space.

Most prefabricated houses he looked at at the time were serviceable, unappealing boxes. Other prefabs that might have fit the bill were still on the drawing board and not yet ready. Refusing to give up, he decided instead to create his own ideal prefab house and enlisted the help, not of an architect but of Mike Kreigel, a rocket scientist who had previously worked with NASA. Kreigel came up with a precision-engineered modular aluminum skeletal frame, which forms the basis of the TomaHouse cabin. The ingenuity of the frame lies in its versatility. Not only can additional add-on modules expand the basic 208-square-foot grid horizontally or vertically, but the core frame also forms a structural support for wide choices of standardized exterior and interior wall, floor, and ceiling panels that can be fastened onto the frame. The interchangeable panels are designed to suit an infinite range of styles, from modern to traditional Bali designs. The patented skeletal frame of interlocking parts is made from high-grade aerospace aluminum, prestressed to withstand forces of up to 2,000 pounds. Additional support and stability is provided by four columns, which are designed to withstand storms and earthquakes and can be sunk into terrain as flexible as sand or rock.

bale classic cabin

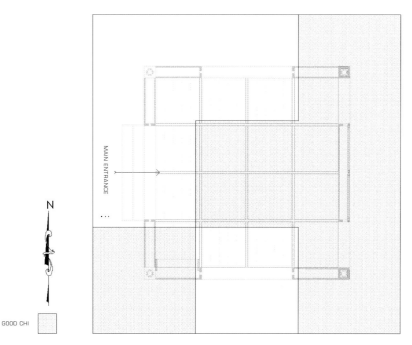

N

GOOD CHI

BALE CLASSIC CABIN, FACING EAST

MAIN ENTRANCE

...

Once Frank Thoma had the structural basis for his house, he turned to Shinta Siregar, an architect trained in Australia and based in Bali. Siregar skillfully distilled and blended indigenous Balinese architecture with modern engineering and conveniences into

OPPOSITE: The elegant bedroom module is beautifully appointed. The layering of materials such as merbau wood, bamboo ceiling panels, lattice screens, and lozenge-shaped woven fiber panels creates a subtle enriched sensual environment. The pitched timber paneled roof dominates the interior, providing cooling ventilation and a sense of spaciousness.

an elegant, luxurious, texturally rich structure that seamlessly unites East and West.

One of the advantages of modular construction is that it allows various individual components to be constructed off-site and subjected to a high degree of quality control before being plugged into the main frame. The Bale Classic Cabin bedroom kit is made up of highly crafted components—from doors and shelves to floors and wall panels. The cabin is defined by a classic Balinese wood-framed shingled pitch roof, which forms an elegant canopy. The sense of ceremony that pervades the small moments of everyday life in Balinese traditional culture is reflected in the measured design of the cabin entrance. The sense of inhabiting a distinct space is emphasized by the two simple steps leading up to a platform patio made from merbau (a versatile hardwood common to Bali) inlaid with stone. A set of wood-trimmed double front glass doors with elegant horn-shaped metal handles slide open to reveal a luxurious interior. Every part of the 208-square-foot space is scrupulously planned out. Alcoves placed just off the entrance on opposite sides of the front door serve as mini foyers that serve as buffers between the abrupt change of space between the exterior and bed. One alcove contains a built-in bookshelf unit while the other stores an electronic control panel that monitors the entertainment system, lighting, and air-conditioning. Tradition and modernity artfully come together in the carved pictographs describing each button's function on the checker board–like control

panel. Just below, a pull-down desk with a stool forms an unobtrusive mini workspace within the bedroom.

The "plug-and-play" character of modular architecture is especially evident in the service areas of the cabin, which were designed as separate modules that are slotted in place on-site. The shower module comes complete with a water heater, exhaust fan, lighting fixtures, and cable and piping attachments. The highly finished bathroom compartment includes a mosaic ceiling panel, granite shower column, and stainless steel shower and tap fixtures. Other sections include the wardrobe, which is fitted with elegant pullout drawers and trays with leather handles; the toilet module comes with an exhaust fan, lighting, and toilet fixtures, and even a toilet paper holder; and the minibar comes complete with lighting fixtures, wine rack, and a fridge.

The modular cabin system opens up a world of choices. In addition to the standard pitch roof, butterfly or flat roof versions are available along with a choice of roof coverings, including shingles, ironwood, tiles, local thatched sirap, solar panels, or a more adventurous elegant tented roof, currently being used in TomaHouse's latest designs for hotel cabins in Africa. A terrace expansion kit includes floor supports, extra wood floor panels, steel balustrades, and a merbau wood railing. The interior walls are lined with a standard wood-framed woven bamboo and lattice partitions. A choice of green silk, timber, and lacquered panels are also available. The Bale

OPPOSITE LEFT and RIGHT: The entryway alcove contains built-in display shelving on one side and on the opposite end a pull-down desk and ebony frame switchboard, which controls all electrical functions. Teak weave lattice panels provide privacy while letting in light and ventilation. ABOVE LEFT: The wood-paneled vanity module is handsomely appointed with a custom-made marble washbasin, elegant tap fixtures, and concealed lighting. ABOVE RIGHT: The elegant shower module complete with a granite column and mosaic ceiling panel was built off-site and plugged into the cabin.

Classic Cabin also comes complete with its designer bedroom furnishing, including the mattress, bedspread, cushions, and bolster as well as a desk chair, tray table, fresco painting, bedside lamps, and other lighting fixtures. For those who live in climates that are less ideal than Bali, there is a range of insulation kits to match a variety of weather situations—from heavy snow and wind to typhoons.

With its core aluminum frame, the flexible, multipurpose Bale Classic Cabin has a wide range of applications, including use as a guesthouse, private residence, poolside cabana, and hotel lodging at luxury remote eco-friendly resorts. The cabin can be assembled in 48 hours by the TomaHouse team anywhere in the world. For individual buyers a fully furnished version of the Bale Classic Cabin costs in the neighborhood of 60,000 Euros, or $77,366, depending on the final package and the location of the site. The company charges a flat rate per house for labor, although basic assembly is relatively easy and do-it-yourself friendly. The kit comes complete with three key tools: a screwdriver, Allen wrench, and wrench.

The cabin also comes complete with a do-it-yourself manual of feng shui formulas to suit a variety of sites. Instructions describe, step-by-step, the proper procedure for bringing good "chi," or energy flow, in your house. A built-in compass is set into the wood floor to aid in the accurate orientation of your home in relation to feng shui principles. Commissioned by TomaHouse from Master Mas Dian, a leading feng

shui expert, the color-coded chart ensures correct placement of beds, sofas, workspace, bathrooms, and other areas of the house. The Feng Shui do-it-yourself manual is a charming touch, reminding us that for all of the certainty of the space-age engineering that supports the TomaHouse cabin, there is still room for mystery and spontaneity. ▪

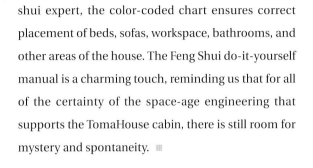

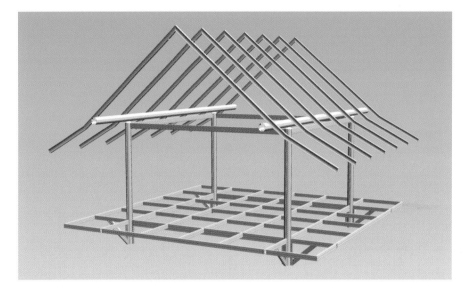

OPPOSITE: The restrained traditional Balinese sitting room pavilion utilizes natural elements such as wood, stone, and fiber. **ABOVE:** The core of the kit house is a lightweight precision-engineered interlocking aluminum frame, which can be expanded vertically and horizontally. **LEFT:** Renderings show the versatility and flexibility of the aluminum frame, which allows for multiple dwellings and works equally well on flat or sloping terrain.

house_o

EXILHÄUSER ARCHITECTS

Energy conservation and affordability are the main principles at work in this unusual underground home created by the Bavaria-based German firm, Exilhäuser Architects. Most architects view nature as a complementary backdrop to be framed and admired. The creators of the underground House_O have a more distinctly utilitarian approach. Here the earth acts as structural insulating element in this carefully considered sustainable housing program.

House_O comes in three sizes: "Mini," "Mid," and "Max." The main semicircular-shaped house is built into a round prefabricated concrete foundation usually used for agricultural cesspools and that Exilhäuser Architects call the "Eco Shell." The hollow cement drum-like core is available in 49-, 57-, and 66-foot widths and the round foundation wall varies in height from 10 to 19 feet depending on the overall house size and number of subterranean floor levels. The Eco Shell's cement walls are sealed with a 5-inch-thick foam thermal insulation layer that greatly assists in retaining warmth. The earth, which

LEFT: House_O's distinctive sunken cement core creates a thermal insulated envelope that preserves temperatures at a constant 39°F. The subterranean post-and-beam house is economical and do-it-yourself friendly. Each dwelling comes with a glass pavilion, which houses all the utilities and provides entry below ground via a staircase.

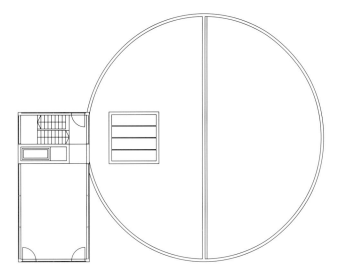

HOUSE_O, ENTRY LEVEL

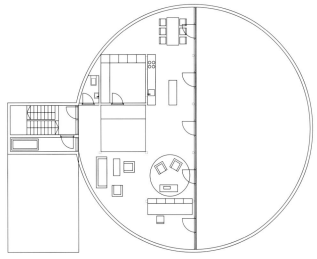

HOUSE_O, FIRST FLOOR

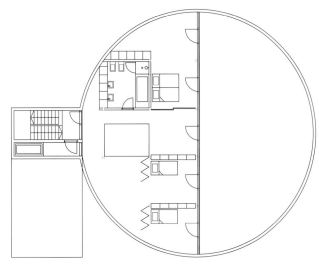

HOUSE_O, SECOND FLOOR

surrounds House_O's cement core, offers the best kind of natural insulation possible. Typical of most underground houses, the temperature remains constant at about 39°F no matter how hot or cold it gets above ground.

The "brain" of House_O, which is responsible for regulating the home's entire energy input and output, is located in a separate glass-walled pavilion called the "Technology Tower." The 322-square-foot pavilion contains a staircase that leads to the subterranean Eco Shell below. The Technology Tower also includes a hot water tank, wastewater pipes, a ventilation system, heat converter, and solar cells on the pavilion roof.

In keeping with the ethic of self-sufficiency, House_O is designed to ensure maximum ease of construction and is specifically promoted as a do-it-yourself project. Designed on an 11-by-11-foot grid, the simple wood-frame beam kit includes standardized wall panels as well as ceiling, window, and floor parts designed to snap into place almost like Lego blocks. The floor plan is fixed but adaptable and uses a series of movable wall partitions that enable the user to make adjustments according to various needs.

The "Mini" version of House_O is comprised of 969 square feet of usable space. Entry to the house occurs via a staircase housed in the Technology Tower located on the ground floor. The glass tower also includes parking space as well as the energy utilities control room. The subterranean first floor area contains an open-plan living, dining, and kitchen area, which is generously illuminated by a bank of floor-to-ceiling windows and sliding doors that span the entire façade of the subterranean floors. A rooftop skylight provides additional illumination throughout the underground living space. The sliding doors, which frame the front elevation, provide adequate ventilation and open onto a semi-circular patio. The subterranean first-floor space combines a bedroom and home office, which can be separated by a movable partition. The House_O service core is efficiently grouped together and consists of a bathroom and laundry room located adjacent to the kitchen. The one-bedroom "Mini" costs an estimated $96,674.

The medium-sized "Mid 120" is 1,291 square feet and is similar in layout to the "Mini" except for an additional self-contained bedroom. A second version of the medium-sized house called the "Mid 240," is greatly enlarged at 2,583 square feet, and includes a two-story underground space complete with an atrium. The entrance to the "Mid 240," like other versions, occurs via the "Technology Tower," pavilion adjacent to the main core. A stairway leads from the ground-floor pavilion down to the subterranean first floor, which contains a bathroom, master bedroom, and two additional smaller bedrooms separated by a living area and atrium. A wall of windows illuminates the entire subterranean first- and second-floor façade with natural light from

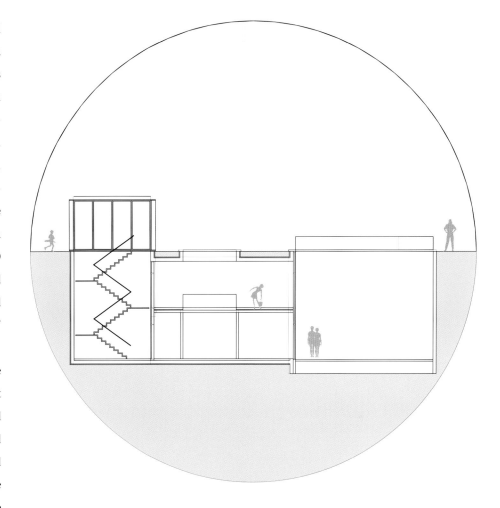

OPPOSITE: The "Max" is the largest in the House_O series. The subterranean first floor contains an open-plan living, dining, and kitchen area and the equally flexible subterranean second-floor bedrooms have movable wall partitions that can be configured in a variety of combinations. ABOVE: House_O's unique entrance pavilion contains a staircase leading below ground.

above. The subterranean second floor contains a home office, and an open-plan living, dining, and kitchen area, which spans the entire front section of the house. Towards the rear of the subterranean second floor space are a half-bathroom and an additional living room adjacent to an atrium, which draws light in from a skylight cut into the sod roof. The "Mid 240" (the 240 stands for the area calculated in square meters) costs $225,614.

Two more versions, dubbed the "Max 150" and the "Max 300," measure 1,614 square feet and 3,229 square feet respectively and have larger spaces and more wall partitions that can be flexibly arranged. The one-story "Max 150" is entered via the "Technology Tower" pavilion staircase, which leads to the subterranean first-floor space containing a living and dining area separated by a movable partition. The subterranean first floor also includes a generous open kitchen space, which overlooks the dining room. At the other end of the house two self-contained bedrooms with movable partitions allow for varying degrees of privacy. The "Max 300" could perhaps be described as the Rolls Royce of the House_O series.

OPPOSITE: The expansive glass windows and sliding doors lets plenty of sunlight into the subterranean first and second floor. A semicircular deck enclosed by the cement foundation wall provides an informal open-air space and ventilation.

The Technology Tower is enlarged to include room for two cars instead of the obligatory one-car garage. The subterranean first floor contains a generous master bedroom and living area, two small bedrooms, a bathroom, and a balcony area overlooking the atrium below. The subterranean second floor contains a dining room and a large living area, which may be enclosed with movable wall partitions. A home office, an additional living room, and an atrium complete the layout. As with other versions, wall-to-ceiling windows span the width of the upper and lower subterranean façade.

House_O is not only energy efficient, it also sits unobtrusively below ground; a visual pollution-free gesture that ensures neighbors' uninterrupted views of the surrounding landscape. Underground houses, apart from being generally energy efficient, are also immune from extreme weather conditions such as tornadoes, freezing temperatures, and hurricanes. With rising energy costs and global competition for increasingly fewer energy resources, Exilhäuser Architects is betting that environmentally smart housing choices will increasingly play a larger role in consumer's home ownership considerations. A far cry from the pessimistic survivalist stereotype of underground houses of past decades, this updated streamlined version is optimistic, light, and airy. As the utopian text of the House_O brochure notes, "it's ecological, it's fast, it's cheap, it saves nature, it changes in time, it's fun, and it fits everyone." ▪

CHAPTER 3

follow that house

building behind the scenes

There is something almost magical about watching a house take shape. Our appetite for watching houses instantly grow in a kind of time-lapse view of home building is enhanced by television's robust remodeling programs like "Extreme Makeover," "Curb Appeal," and "Weekend Warriors" in which new houses and new lives seem to spring up in an hour or less—commercials notwithstanding. None of the interest in do-it-yourself remodeling and home building would be possible without prefabricated materials and innovative construction techniques, which require less skilled labor and save time. The following images show how steel components and structural insulated panels are opening up new possibilities for housing, while pushing us to think beyond the box.

Residence: BRANFORD POINT, Branford, Connecticut

Architecture Firm: FACE Design

Kit of Parts:
13 post-tensioned moment frames
115 structural insulated panels (SIPs)
specialty prefabricated components: stairs, railings,
        partitions, lighting, and furniture

Construction Time: 29 Weeks

A flatbed truck delivers the prefabricated structural insulated panels, which are efficiently unloaded at the building site.

Premanufactured hollow tube sections and structural arches are bolted together and laid out in preparation to be hoisted into place.

The first of thirteen steel arch frames is hoisted upright and firmly bolted to connectors embedded in the cement foundation floor.

Nearly completely raised, the sturdy steel-ribbed skeletal frame is given additional strength using horizontal I beams.

The outline of the house begins to take shape as flat and curved prefabricated structural insulated panels form the outer skin. Three hundred custommade clips were used to secure the structural insulated panels in between the steel ribs.

The structural insulated panels have precut window openings and form a virtually airtight skin that traces the peaks and eaves of the sloping roofline. Cross braces provide the framework for the mezzanine floor.

The exterior elevation is clad in Ipe ironwood siding and stucco. The sloping steel roof is powder-coated and galvanized for extra protection and durability.

CHAPTER 4

a consumer guide

buying a kit house

There are many reasons to opt for a prefabricated kit house as opposed to the conventional stick-built variety created from scratch. One main reason is cost; houses that are packaged in a kit tend to be cheaper than conventional housing. They need fewer skilled laborers and are often erected in a much shorter timeframe. Many modern kit houses embrace principles of mass-customization, allowing the consumer greater choice than ever before. There are flexible floor plans and styles to suit nearly every budget and living situation and designs often come with built-in possibilities for future expansion. Design quality is an important issue to consider as well. Whether you choose to buy a modern kit home from a manufacturer or direct from an architect, today's packaged houses offer an alternative to the mundane developer-driven cookie-cutter homes on the market. With a kit home, choice and design excellence are not necessarily indexed to wealth. As the kits featured in this volume show, innovative, good design is possible without investing the kind of time and cost required by traditional stick-built custom homes.

modern kit home methods

Although there are hybrid kits that incorporate more than one building system into their design, many of the modern kit homes featured in this book fall into one of three construction styles: Modular, post-and-beam frames, or panelized building systems. The benefits of each method of construction are explored below.

Modular Kit Homes offer the most integrated form of housing construction available. Instead of hundreds of separate parts put together on-site, factory methods of modular construction make it possible for parts to be put together in a factory. A modular kit of parts is more likely to arrive in huge chunks—whole walls and roof sections, even bathrooms and kitchen modules that can be "plugged-in" within the confines of the factory. The entire outer shell of a home is often produced entirely indoors and often come prewired with plumbing preinstalled. The partially or fully constructed exterior shell can be shipped to the work site or as a complete shell and lowered onto the permanent foundation by crane. Often whole exteriors or outer housing shells can be erected in as little as a day, allowing interior finishing to take place as a do-it-yourself project or using professional builders. Advantages of modular construction are as follows:

- Because modular houses are built indoors at a factory, they are less subject to weather delays and are subject to factory inspections and quality control. They are faster and cheaper than conventional buildings, which are subject to the vagaries of weather. Since they are constructed essentially in a factory and trucked to site, they require less on-site labor.

- If you are lucky enough to have a small urban or suburban lot conveniently close to a major city center, you may want to consider a factory-built modular home. The factory-made exterior shell can often be lowered quickly and efficiently on-site.

Courtyard patio, Flatpak House, Minneapolis, Minnesota, designed by Lazor Office

- For small lots, modular homes allow for vertical expansion. Modules can add to the existing structure later, as the family expands or more space is needed. In situations where the environment is fragile and a small footprint is required, modular building methods offer a relatively unobtrusive way of environmentally controlled construction.

- Because they have to be transported to their destination, modular homes are often constructed to be stronger and sturdier than conventional homes. Joints are often nailed and glued for extra measure.

- For do-it-yourself homebuilders, modular housing offers a less formidable challenge, since the outer shell of the house arrives intact with wiring and plumbing preinstalled and placed on-site for you.

Post-and-Beam Precut Kits have more parts than modular versions and tend to be more expensive to build because, quite simply, with many more parts they require more labor and management on-site. Precut homes though do offer more variety in terms of construction styles, from A-frames to pole systems. Precut kits are also more easily transportable in smaller containers, and can be shipped with greater ease to far away destinations. Advantages of precut homes are as follows:

- Precut homes use post-and-beam construction methods, which structurally support expansive interiors spaces, making airy, open, light-filled rooms.

- Post-and-beam precut homes can support huge glass window-walls and are perfect for large plots of land, with bucolic views.

- Lumber used in precut homes are of the highest quality comprising of kiln-dried timbers, which settle well without warping or shrinking.

- Precut homes use several different systems of construction and therefore offer greater flexibility in terms of design. Difficult and complex spatial requirements are often easier to incorporate.

Panelized Home Kits are becoming increasingly popular in home building. Not only are they sturdy, but also they provide excellent insulation. There are generally two types of panels: open and closed. Open panels do not have any insulation or finishing material attached and are often comprised of just a single exterior sheathing, leaving the interior wall exposed. Closed panels are both insulated and finished on the inside. Structural insulated panels (SIPs) are closed panels more completely finished and are made up of foam sandwiched between two sheets of oriented strand board. Advantages of panelized kit homes are as follows:

- Panelized homes are extremely energy efficient and provide superior insulation.

- The exterior shell of panelized kits can be assembled in days, allowing interior work to proceed even while other parts of the house are being finished.

- Quick assembly saves time and money.

- Panelized kits allow for more flexible floor plans and custom design input compared to modular homes.

research

If you are thinking of purchasing a kit house, the best initial investment you can make is to devote as much time to research as possible. A look on the Internet alone reveals many modern architecture firms with eye-catching prototypes and plans in the works to develop kit houses. However, only a handful of firms actually have homes currently in production or have partnerships with larger kit home manufacturers that can provide you with a full range of services. Do enough research to familiarize yourself with what is currently available as well as basic building methods. From trade associations and various non-profit homeowner organizations to specialist modern architecture websites and magazines, there is a wealth of information that can help you decide which are the best modern kits available to suit your needs. There are even blogs that detail homeowner's experiences, which are worth looking at to balance out sometimes overly enthusiastic marketing copy by kit manufacturers. Attend as many kit open houses as possible in addition to a particular house you have in mind. Not only will you learn more, you will also gain better understanding of a potential home if you can compare it with the competition.

finding the right plot of land

These days it is getting harder to find a good plot of land. If you are not lucky enough to own a suburban plot or even a derelict urban brownfield site, you may have to move further away from city centers. Before you buy your kit house make sure you have made the right choice of land and you are comfortable with the surrounding environment. Plot brokers can be very helpful. Generally, land should assume no more than thirty-five percent of your budget. Below is a checklist of things to consider before you choose.

- Are you an acceptable distance from decent health facilities, hospitals, clinics, or doctors?

- Does your area have adequate police, ambulance, and fire services? Is it close to dangerous high-traffic highways? Make sure your plot is well away from excessive smoke, noise, and other potentially hazardous pollution.

- Are there adequate cultural, religious, and educational institutions nearby such as schools, colleges, museums, libraries, community colleges, or churches?

- Are there any visible signs of future growth and development such as parks, roads, offices, or residential buildings?

- If the price of your land is too good to be true, check its history. Make sure there are no underlying problems such as pollution or potential extra costs for sewage disposal, blasting, or other issues.

choosing the site

▣ At best, land should have a slight gradient so that water drains away not towards the home.

▣ Soil should have great absorption. For example, sandy loam is better than clay, which is less absorbent.

▣ It is preferable to choose land with public water and sewage services rather than paying extra costs for a well or septic tank.

▣ Hire a qualified surveyor to do a general assessment. A personal recommendation is always best, although often the engineering department at a local university may have a qualified surveyor on staff who freelances.

environmental considerations

▣ Make sure your kit home uses environmentally sound green insulation materials wherever possible. Double or triple glazing can help and offers effective insulation that helps energy costs. Think of incorporating a green roof into your design for added insulation.

▣ Design your home with strategically placed windows and a southern orientation to make the most of passive solar energy. Also seek other solutions such as solar panels or geothermal heating.

▣ Where possible select environmentally sustainable materials such as bamboo flooring, green-approved solvents or paints, or natural roofing materials such as slate. Shingles and tiles made from recycled material may be used.

financing

Before buying land, it is best to approach your lending institution with a thorough and detailed building program that includes a description and preliminary plan of your home along with a detailed budget. In addition you should be familiar with your local area building codes. While it seems like a lot of trouble to amass as much information as possible, it will provide your lending institution with useful information and prevent you from spending more money than is necessary before you know if you will obtain a loan or not. It is worthwhile to build in an emergency cushion of around ten percent to your budget.

To build a kit house, often two kinds of loans are needed: one is short-term and pays for the construction phase, including materials and labor. The other is a mortgage that pays for the construction loan once the house is completed. Some banks combine the two, though to obtain a construction loan, you will need detailed specific building plans as well as a detailed budget, a site report, a resume detailing your (if you choose the do-it-yourself route) or your contractor's building experience.

the kit house checklist

Most kit house manufacturers offer a full range of services to ease the construction process. Some of the larger companies even provide a detailed workbook or construction plan. Following are some important elements to consider before you decide to purchase a kit home.

- Before any materials or sections begin to arrive make sure you, your project manager, or builder understand the delivery process step-by-step, especially what happens once material is unloaded.

- Make sure the manufacturer has conducted a site inspection prior to deliveries, especially if you have a complex site. The manufacturer's project manager should be able to identify difficulties getting to the site, such as low bridges, narrow roads, tight bends, and overhanging tree branches. Every conceivable problem along the route should be noted and discussed ahead of time.

- Work out in advance if any special equipment will be required such as cranes or internal or external scaffolding. Confirm whether you or the manufacturer will be responsible for supplying extra equipment.

- Ensure that you or your designated builder/manager have a product list noting all the materials brought to the site. The manufacturer should include a reasonable amount of extra parts to account for wastage.

- Hire a steel storage container or use an existing barn, shed, or garage as a secure, dry place to store materials. Storage is especially needed for precut kits. Make sure items such as doors, windows, joinery, adhesives, and boards are stored safely and properly. Ask your manufacturer or check the housing manual for instructions on how to store material, especially vulnerable pieces such as wood flooring, staircases, and other prefinished items.

- Make sure there are adequate bathroom facilities for building workers to use on-site. If your site is in a remote location and there are no facilities close by, you may have to hire a portable chemical toilet.

- Once the shell of the house has been completed, the kit manufacturer's project manager should take you and your contractor on a thorough inspection of construction so far. The manufacturer's project manager should also take you and your contractor through the remaining amount of work to be done.

- Confirm what aspects of the site are your responsibility and what equipment you have to provide, such as scaffolding, ladders, rubbish containers, electricity, and tarpaulins.

- Make sure you or your contractor gets a very detailed schedule of the entire building program from start to finish.

- Clarify the extent of your liability and make sure you or your chosen kit manufacturer have appropriate coverage to protect you and anyone else present on the site. In addition, ensure that your kit house is protected against all risks such as fire, vandalism, weather, and all other eventualities. If you are planning to undertake any aspect of construction yourself, make sure you have personal injury insurance.

sources

websites + blogs

Whether you are considering buying a prefabricated kit house or would like more information, the following sources are indispensable, and should be among the first places you consult.

Live Modern

www.livemodern.com
From blogs written by prefab homeowners, complete with detailed entries about the process of purchasing and installing a prefabricated home, to news about the latest prefab houses, chat forums, support services, and in-depth resource listings, Live Modern is an impressive one-stop-shop website for information on prefab homes.

Fabprefab

www.fabprefab.com
The most comprehensive list of modern prefabricated home designs available.

Dwell Magazine

www.dwellmag.com
The website of the pioneering magazine devoted to modern housing and design is full of informative features on important prefabricated modern home projects.

Land + Living

www.landliving.com
A website devoted to modern architecture and design.

Luminhaus

www.luminhaus.com
mail@luminhaus.com
Designed by architect Rocio Romero, Luminhaus is the first LV House kit purchased. The two-bedroom, one bath, modern mountain retreat set in the mountains of Amherst Virginia is available for rent as a vacation home.

MoCo Loco Modern Contemporary Design

www.mocoloco.com
A web magazine devoted to modern contemporary design with profiles of the latest prefab architecture.

Royal Homes

www.royalhomestoronto.typepad.com
Website by Royal Homes, Canada's largest modular homebuilder. Comprehensive website includes information about Royal Homes Q Series modern modular house. Also includes a wide range of articles, links, and photography on designer prefab homes.

The Home Blog

www.thehomeblog.blogs.com
Repository for information on buying and selling a home, interior decoration, landscaping, and new trends in home design.

Treehugger

www.treehugger.com
Website devoted to sustainable energy issues including information on the latest environmentally friendly architecture and design

architects

Bauart Architekten Bern

Fruchthof
Laupenstrasse 20
3008 Bern, Switzerland
41-31-385-15-15
(fax) 41-31-385-15-10
www.bauart.ch
bauart@bauart.ch

Exilhäuser Architekten

Hauptstrasse 19
83539 Pfaffing, Germany
49-8076-88-66-80
(fax) 49-8076-88-66-81
www.exilhaeuser.de

FACE Design

225 North 7th Street
Brooklyn, New York 11211
718-486-8288
(fax) 718-486-8339
www.facedesign.com

Kalkin & Company

Adam Kalkin
59-65 Mine Brooke Road
Bernardsville, New Jersey 07924
908-696-1999
(fax) 908-969-1998
www.architectureandhygiene.com

Lazor Office

3236 California Street NE
Minneapolis, Minnesota 55418
612-788-5355
(fax) 612-788-5357
www.flatpakhouse.com

Lindal Reflection Homes
1-888-4LINDAL
www.lindal.com

Matteo Thun
Via Appiani 9
I-20121 Milan Italy
39-02-655691
(fax) 39-02-6570646
www.matteothun.com

Michelle Kaufmann Designs
www.mkarchitecture.com
www.glidehouse.com

NowHouse
415-344-0806
www.nowhouse.org

Office of Mobile Design
Jennifer Siegal
1725 Abbot Kinney Boulevard
Venice, California 90291
310-439-1129
(fax) 310-439-2495
www.designmobile.com

Resolution: 4 Architecture
Joseph Tanney and Robert Luntz
150 West 28th Street, Suite 1902
New York, New York 10001
212-675-9266
(fax) 212-206-0944
www.re4a.com

Rocio Romero, LLC
PO Box 30
Perryville, Missouri 63775
314-367-7736
www.rocioromero.com
sales@rocioromero.com

Royal Homes Modern
213 Arthur Street
Wingham, Ontario, Canada N0G 2W0
416-346-5738 or 1-800-265-3083
(fax) 519-357-1742
www.royalhomestoronto.com
brochures@royalhomes.com

Studio Aisslinger
Oranienplatz 4
D-10999 Berlin, Germany
49-30-315-05-400
(fax) 49-30-315-05-401
www.loftcube.net
info@loftcube.net

Taalman Koch Architecture
2404 Wilshire Boulevard #11F
Los Angeles, California 91204
213-380-1060
(fax) 213-380-1260
www.tkithouse.com
alan@tkarchitecture.com

Tekton Architecture Incorporated
771 Clementina Street
San Francisco, California 94103
415-863-2232
(fax) 415-863-2236
www.tektonarchitecture.com
info@tektonarchitecture.com

TomaHouse Marketing, S.L.
Paseo Maritimo Camino de Atall 27
12579 Alcossebre
Castellon, Spain
34-964-413-103
www.tomahouse.com
saleseurope@tomahouse.com

WeberHaus
www.weberhaus.de

The weeHouse
www.weehouses.com
info@weehouses.com

suppliers

The following suppliers are mentioned in the various kit houses featured in the book. Because of their flexible and highly adaptable designs, many of the products work particularly well with the slim line, compact modern aesthetic of many contemporary prefabricated kit houses.

American Standard
www.americanstandard-us.com

Hülsta
www.huelsta.com

Andersen Windows
www.andersenwindows.com

Ingo Maurer
www.ingo-maurer.com

Bulthaup
www.bulthaup.com

Interlubke
www.interlubke.com

Cappellini
www.cappellini.it

KitchenAid
www.kitchenaid.com

DuPont Corian
www.corian.com

Kohler
www.kohler.com

Duravit
www.duravit.com

Loewen
www.loewen.com

Flor
www.interfaceflor.com

Philippe Starck
www.philippe-starck.com

Gaggenau
www.gaggenau.com

Reveal Designs
www.reveal-designs.com

GE Appliances
www.geappliances.com

Toto
www.totousa.com

Hostaglas
www.accessplastics.com

Viking
www.vikingrange.com

credits

Living room, Modular 1 House, Kansas City, Missouri, designed by Studio 804

index